THE Rainbow of God's Creation

LGBTIQA+ Realities and Catholicism

Trish Hindmarsh

garratt
PUBLISHING

Published in Australia by
Garratt Publishing
32 Glenvale Crescent
Mulgrave, VIC 3170
www.garrattpublishing.com.au

Copyright in this work remains the property of the contributing authors.
Copyright © Trish Hindmarsh 2025

All rights reserved. Except as provided by the Australian copyright law, no part of this book may be reproduced in any way without permission in writing from the publisher.

Cover and Text Design by Guy Holt
Edited by Greg Hill
Cover image © iStock FG Trade1894598617
Photographs © iStock (pp references) p I FG Trade1894598617, p 13 limeart 2166754777, p 14 enjoynz 2061291966, pp 15–16 FG Trade 1894598619, p 22 limeart 2166754777, p 23, enjoynz 2061291966, p 33 Wirestock 1432199118, p 34 enjoynz 2061291966, p 40 iStock-483930188, p 40 mason01 483930188, p 53 enjoynz 2061291966, limeart 2166754777, p 55 BrianAJackson 477843515, p 54–55 EyeEm Mobile GmbH 2166855779, p 62 limeart 2166754777, enjoynz 2061291966, p 65 limeart 2166754777, p 66 enjoynz 2061291966, p 70 limeart 2166754777, p 71 PeopleImages1132222242, p 82 limeart 2166754777, p 84 enjoynz 2061291966, pp 86–87 Mike_Pellinni 490758980, p 88 InnaFelker 918511938, p 89 MWayOut 2222749774, p 92 blinow61 2107382054, p 94 franswillemblok 1177822270, p 96 limeart 2166754777, p 97 enjoynz 2061291966, p 98–99 1204295717 MasterLu, p 100–101 DrAfter123 1127355447 , p 112 Charnchai 1227131479, limeart 2166754777, p 113 enjoynz 2061291966, p 126 limeart 2166754777, LindaMarieB160104165, p 127 enjoynz 2061291966, p 131 Unaihuiziphotography 1476508856
Photographs © provided by author p 9–10, p 15, p 26, p 36, p 60, p 68, pp 74–75, pp 78–80, p 91, p 104, pp 106–107, p 109, pp 116–117, p 119
Illustration © Alamy p 31 Council of Jerusalem, a conference of the Christian Apostles in Jerusalem, scene of the New Testament, Histoire Biblique de L'Ancien Testament

Scripture quotations are drawn from the New Revised Standard Version of the Bible, copyright © 1989 by the Division of Christian Education of the National Council of the Churches of Christ in the USA. Used by permission. All rights reserved.

ISBN 9781923095267

Cataloguing in Publication information for this title is available from the National Library of Australia.
www.nla.gov.au

The authors and publisher gratefully acknowledge the permission granted to reproduce the copyright material in this book. Every effort has been made to trace copyright holders and to obtain their permission for the use of copyright material.

It is rare to see such a well-written, straightforward, pastoral and unashamedly Catholic introduction to one of the Church's best kept, but now emerging, secrets. But in addition, this little book is suffused with joy, making it very special indeed.

James Alison is a Catholic theologian, priest, author and global teacher.
He is committed to the recognition and pastoral care of LGBTIQA+ people as images of God and variations within humanity, reflecting the diversity of God' Creation.

The Church is seeking a new engagement with people who identify as LGBTQIA+ and who often feel rejected by the Church. It's not easy to see the way forward, but the journey starts with the ear. We are in search of a new kind of listening to the voices of people who identify as LGBTQIA+. The Church needs to listen to what these, our sisters and brothers, judge to be the truth of their experience. Only once we have listened deeply can we enter into the dialogue that will carry us forward under the influence of the Holy Spirit. How to respond to what we hear from people who identify as LGBTQIA+ and yet be faithful to the Church's understanding of the human person: that's the challenge we face. In what is offered here, Trish Hindmarsh helps us take a step in the right direction on the long journey of dialogue.

Mark Coleridge is Archbishop Emeritus in Brisbane
He is also a theologian, scripture scholar, pastor and teacher.
He is a former Chair of the Australian Catholic Bishops Conference.

> Pope Francis wrote, 'Discernment is a grace from God, but it requires our human involvement...'

Using the Guide

The Guide is intended for individual reflection or for use in a group setting to facilitate discernment through dialogue, leading to greater understanding, conversion of heart, and action. The final document from the Synod on Synodality (2024) leaves us in no doubt that Synodality is a 'constitutive dimension' of the Church, not an option.

The opportunities for Reflection, Prayerful Conversations and Shared Prayer, offered throughout the Guide are an invitation to practise the 'synodal' way of 'walking together' towards greater understanding and faith-inspired action.

Pope Francis wrote, 'Discernment is a grace from God, but it requires our human involvement in simple ways: *praying, reflecting, paying attention to one's inner disposition, listening and talking to one another in an authentic, meaningful, and welcoming way.*'

(For a Synodal Church: Communion, Participation, and Mission, 2.2. Vademecum for the Synod on Synodality, 2021.)

LGBTIQA+ Glossary of Common Terms

In this Guide the acronym LGBTIQA+ is used throughout unless quoting from a particular source that favours a different acronym, for example LGBTQ; LGBT or LGBTQIA+. The following offers a descriptor for each of the letters and the symbol in 'LGBTIQA+'.

Asexual: a sexual orientation that reflects little to no sexual attraction, either within or outside relationships.

Bisexual: an individual who is sexually and/or romantically attracted to people of the same gender and people of another gender.

Gay: an individual who identifies as a man and is sexually and/or romantically attracted to other people who identify as men. The term gay can also be used in relation to women who are sexually and romantically attracted to other women.

Intersex: an umbrella term that refers to individuals who have anatomical, chromosomal and hormonal characteristics that differ from medical and conventional understandings of male and female bodies.

Lesbian: an individual who identifies as a woman and is sexually and/or romantically attracted to other people who identify as women.

Queer: a term sometimes used to describe a range of sexual orientations and gender identities, in former times often a derogatory term.

Transgender/Trans: umbrella terms used to refer to people whose assigned sex at birth does not match their gender identity.

+ (Plus) *Represents others not included here.*[1]

---

[1] Based on The Australian Institute of Family Studies comprehensive listing and description of terms used in relation to LGBTIQA+ realities. Found at the LGBTIQA+ glossary of common terms, Australian Institute of Family Studies, aifs.gov.au, October 30, 2024.

Contents

Preface 1

Foreword 3

Introduction 5

Chapter 1 17
Why has the Church been so slow to change?

Chapter 2 57
The tide is turning: Signs of Catholic support for LGBTIQA+ people

Chapter 3 87
The 'Rainbow': Symbol and Spectrum

Chapter 4 101
Where to from here for the Catholic Church?

Acknowledgements 129

Bibliography 130

"

The significance of the 'rainbow' ... is explained as a beautiful, shared symbol of promise and fidelity...

+ Vincent Long Van Nguyen, OFM Conv.
Bishop of Parramatta, Australia

Preface

This book sets out to explore existing Catholic teaching and responses to LGBTIQA+ people and their realities. Scriptural sources that are often evoked in support of teaching that describes gay and lesbian people as 'aberrations' and their expressions of sexuality as 'always sinful' are challenged through the lens of theological, scientific, and scriptural scholarship.

The history of persecution of gay and lesbian people is shown to be very real, as is the compassion of faith-filled Catholics who have defended and supported them – especially since the AIDS crisis.

The late Pope Francis met, listened to, and even befriended LGBTIQA+ people during his papacy, and his respectful engagement is shown to have ushered in a new pastoral approach for the Church from the highest levels of authority.

The testimonies and hopes of Catholics nationally and globally through the Australian Plenary Council and the Synod on Synodality offered relevant data from around the Catholic world, on a scale never previously possible. This data demonstrated that Catholics want their Church to seriously research and discern just and Christ-like responses to this reality. Catholic agencies founded during the past sixty years for LGBTIQA+ support and ministry around the world are introduced in the book.

The significance of the 'Rainbow' – both scripturally and for LGBTIQA+ identity – is explained as a beautiful, shared symbol of promise and fidelity. New learning, shared story-telling, and prayerful conversation are offered as ways to discern how best Catholic faith can commit to engage in more authentic relationships with LGBTIQA+ people.

This user-friendly resource is intended for educators, parishes, pastors, leaders, families and senior students. The call of the Holy Spirit is extended to open the readers' hearts and arms to those of our human siblings who belong to what renowned theologian and gay priest, Fr James Alison, refers to as a 'minority variant' within humanity. That is, people who are different in sexual orientation from the majority, but equal in dignity within the ambit of the loving God's Creation.

– + Vincent Long Van Nguyen, OFM Conv.
Bishop of Parramatta, Australia

Foreword

In early 2024, at the invitation of Rainbow Catholics Australia, I attended their 'Inter-Agency' meeting as a 'straight' person, listening and learning in preparation for drafting this Guide. Their commitment to be true to themselves and to their Catholic Faith, the source of sacramental 'graces' they rely on from their 'spiritual home', touched me more deeply than I can say. The experience galvanised me to begin this work, and profoundly alerted me to the urgency for their voices to be heard and believed by the Catholic Church.

The last encyclical from Pope Francis *Dilexit Nos* ('He Loved Us'), was published during the writing of this guide and struck me like lightening as a timely grace from God – for myself, for the Church and for humanity, as we respond to what Pope Francis recognised as a 'change of era', united within the Sacred Heart of Jesus. Francis wrote:

> The heart is the locus of sincerity, where deceit and disguise have no place. It usually indicates our true intentions, what we really think, believe and desire, the 'secrets' that we tell no one: in a word, the naked truth about ourselves. It is the part of us that is neither appearance nor illusion, but is instead authentic, real, entirely 'who we are'.
>
> Pope Francis, *Dilexit Nos* (5), 2024

I have also been energised by the motto of the Sisters of Charity, *'Caritas Christo ugit nos'* ("The love of Christ impels us") in attempting to write this Guide. The Sisters were among the first Catholics in Australia to publicly recognise and honour the human dignity of gay men, as we see in the Introduction.

Dialogue with LGBTIQA+ people

Pope Francis demonstrated that there is much to discover from open-hearted dialogue with LGBTIQA+ people regarding the limitless love of God, expressed in the diverse gifts of Creation. There remains much for the Catholic Church to learn about the human struggle they daily face for justice and full recognition of their humanity, wherever bigotry and ignorance are allowed to continue. We can open our eyes and hearts to those who identify as 'Rainbow' people, seeing them as gifts of God's infinite creativity and our 'siblings' within the human family. They too are invited to share the 'Feast' in the Kingdom Christ Jesus came to announce.

– Trish Hindmarsh, September 2025

Introduction

It was 1982 and a typical morning recess break at Marcellin College Randwick. The well-loved no-nonsense female music teacher, mother of five grown children, shared with me some headline news she had heard on the ABC before work. Una was a woman of deep faith and serious concern for young people. She had heard that an epidemic called HIV/AIDS,[1] reportedly spread by active homosexual men, was sweeping the US and Europe, and would without a shadow of doubt infect Australia. This was shocking news that promised to rock the western world.

Una was a woman who could conduct a thousand male voices at a school Mass, almost bringing the parish Church down as their voices rang, 'So I leave my boats behind! Leave them on familiar shores! Set my heart upon the deep! Follow you again, my Lord!'[2] A rousing song well suited for camaraderie and liturgical expression in a beach suburb where the best friend of every second young man was his surfboard.

---

[1] HIV/AIDS Human immunodeficiency virus (HIV) is a virus that attacks the body's immune system. Acquired immunodeficiency syndrome (AIDS) occurs at the most advanced stage of infection. World Health Organisation definitions. Found at: https://www.who.int/news-room/fact-sheets/detail/hiv-aids

[2] Galilee Song, Frank Anderson MSC, 1981.

At this time, and not far from this scene, the notorious taunting, hunting down and murder of several gay men along the cliffs of the eastern suburbs made headline news. The AIDS epidemic caused great fear and panic across the nation, a rehearsal of sorts for COVID some forty years later. Fear, recrimination and bigotry against what would later become known as the LGBTIQA+ community was rife at the time in many families, work places and social gatherings, greatly exacerbated by the AIDS crisis.

Since colonial times, Australian law had classed homosexuality as illegal until this came to be challenged in the late 1970's and finally overturned in all Australian states and territories by 1997.

Catholicism's teaching – that all sexual acts outside a lawful monogamous marriage between a man and a woman are immoral and against the 'Natural Law' – confirmed LGBTIQA+ Catholics in a position of condemnation and exclusion. All too often this exclusion extended within families. Other faiths were in a similar position.

There was and still is much 'leaving of boats behind' and 'setting of hearts upon the deep' to be done for the Church to fully embrace LGBTIQA+ people as innately children of God created in God's loving image and likeness.

> 'Our attitude was one of loving the person with no condemnation. It was as simple as that,' she said. 'We were often asked why we chose to look after them and our response was always the same, "Why wouldn't you?" We walked alongside so many men as they died, which taught me love is all that really matters.'
>
> Sister Clare Nolan RSC

INTRODUCTION

Light in the darkness: St Vincent's Hospital

Bigotry, ignorance and persecution of gay men during the height of the AIDS epidemic did nothing to deter the Sisters of Charity at St Vincent's Hospital in Darlinghurst from setting up a facility, known as 'Ward 17', for the treatment of AIDS victims.

Their work is immortalised in an article by Debbie Cramsie:[3]

> It was a time of great loss but even greater love. Forty years ago, the first HIV/AIDS case was diagnosed in Australia amid a climate of fear, hysteria, and uncertainty. Young men were being admitted to Ward 17 South at St Vincent's Hospital at an alarming rate. Most never left. Ward 17 South was the only dedicated HIV/AIDS ward in the country. It was often described as a war zone, with conditions similar to battlefield nursing. The work was incredibly tough. There were always too few beds and too many patients, no known treatment, and the suffering indescribable. Personal protection equipment (PPE) was unheard of but very quickly introduced, which would later pave the way for the management of the COVID-19 pandemic. The Sisters of Charity who staffed St Vincent's were called saints by those in their care and lived out their charism of ministering to the marginalised, poor and sick in the face of hostility. Colleagues and hospital staff treated them with fear and apprehension, they received criticism from the wider society, and condemnation from within the church. Yet without the sisters' witness, thousands of men – many ostracised by their own families – would have died alone and uncared for. Retired Director of Nursing at St Vincent's Hospital, Sister Clare Nolan RSC, reflected that while it was a 'very, very difficult time' it was also filled with love. Referred to as 'the lepers of our time', she said caring for the men on Ward 17 South was a 'privilege' and a chance

---

[3] Article, 'Museum honours Sisters' service during Australian AIDS epidemic,' article in *Catholic Weekly*, Sydney, 1 Mar., 2023.

> My partner Brian and I had a small farm at the time; it was ideal for us all to administer to him. When he died, I was cradling him in my arms, he went in such a peaceful way with our love surrounding him. He had received the Eucharist and Anointing from a wonderful Vincentian priest before he moved to be with us at the farm.

From a gay Catholic man, sharing how he had nursed his brother dying of HIV/AIDS.

INTRODUCTION

Retired Director of Nursing at St Vincent's Hospital, Sister Clare Nolan RSC with David Polson, one of the first men to be diagnosed with HIV/AIDS in Australia. Used with permission. Permission for photo granted by the Sisters of Charity Australia.

to practise true Ignatian spirituality. 'Our attitude was one of loving the person with no condemnation. It was as simple as that,' she said. 'We were often asked why we chose to look after them and our response was always the same, "Why wouldn't you?" We walked alongside so many men as they died, which taught me love is all that really matters.'[4]

The founding of *Acceptance*

While this trail-blazing healthcare work was being established at St Vincent's Hospital in the 1980's, most Catholics had no idea that Catholic lay group, Acceptance, had been founded in Sydney (1972),

---

[4] Permission granted to cite these details by Sr Clare Nolan RSC, David Polson, sole survivor of the men in Ward 17, and the Sisters of Charity Leadership Team. Granted and received with gratitude, Nov 1, 2024. Their story was also featured in The Australian Women's Weekly, December 2024, as the article, 'A Mission of Love' by Susan Chenery.

offering some hope and solace to Catholic gay men and women. As their website explains:

> ... a group of gay men and women began meeting in each other's houses for a monthly Mass. Priests were invited to celebrate this Mass, sometimes travelling long distances. At that time, it was difficult for gay and lesbian Catholics to participate openly in the church, but the priests at these Masses preached a gospel message that welcomed gays and lesbians as loved people of God.[5]

There were prophetic priests, nuns, and Catholic lay people who were leading the way before it was even legal, let alone accepted, to be gay.

HIV/AIDS Catholic Ministry: Parramatta Diocese 1986

Catholic Priest John Girdauskas shared with me his experience in ministry with men affected with HIV/AIDS and their families during

---

[5] Acceptance Website, accessed March, 2024 at: https://www.gaycatholic.com.au/history

INTRODUCTION

the 1980s.[6] In the newly formed Parramatta Diocese (1986), the first Bishop, Bede Heather, together with Sr Catherine Ryan RSM, saw a need in Western Sydney and founded HIV/AIDS Catholic Ministry. The ministry was based in a rented, five-bedroom house in Blacktown, known as 'Bethany'. Fr John was appointed as Chaplain and Sr Catherine as Director. Bethany offered refuge to gay men who needed respite, cared for by a full-time live-in carer. This outreach operated in collaboration with other local and non-government health agencies. John and Catherine arranged funerals for those who died of HIV/AIDS-related illness.

These accounts of ministry to gay people are examples of how the Church is called to respond in love and compassion as a 'field hospital' (the celebrated phrase of Pope Francis), ministering to those 'who suffer, or are in any way afflicted', as the Vatican II document *Gaudium et Spes* ('Joy and Hope') stated in its opening clarion call.[7] Those 'afflicted' includes those who contracted and died from complications of the HIV/AIDS virus, and those who have suffered and continue to suffer bigotry and persecution in many countries because they identify as other than heterosexual.

Learning from the past

It is important for it to be known that there were Catholics who recognised the implications for pastoral ministry of the growing HIV/AIDS crisis, responding with compassion to the plight of their gay and lesbian fellow humans at a time when society could arrest them for not being heterosexual. Those creative actions were new and challenging for the mainstream Church of the time, and remain so for the contemporary Catholic Church. They were early responses by Catholic followers of Christ to one of the key 'Signs of the Times' in the 20th and 21st centuries – namely, the growing awareness in society of the human dignity and rights of LGBTIQA+ people.

---

[6] Author interview with Fr John Girdauskas, Burnie, March 15, 2024.
[7] *Gaudium et Spes*, par. 1, Documents of Vatican II, edited by Abbott, W M, published by Geoffrey Chapman, London, 1966.

Catholic Social Teachings are modern interpretations of the Gospels, and honour the basic dignity and rights of all humans, endorsing their enshrinement in the Universal Declaration of Human Rights (1948). The Church has failed to apply this great body of Catholic teaching to LGBTIQA+ realities, despite having been a global leader in drawing on them to defend the rights of workers, the Indigenous dispossessed of their culture, those condemned by injustice to live in poverty and disadvantage, or those ravaged by war or family violence.

In Chapter 2, we see how Pope Francis remained open to learn from and embrace LGBTIQA+ people. He knew their pain and he made a point of meeting them face-to-face to listen, to learn and express his love for them. He saw dialogue with them as part of his commitment to 'go to the peripheries', to 'get out of the sacristy and into the streets'[8]. He stopped short of changing official Church teaching that 'all homosexual acts are intrinsically disordered'[9]. However, he allowed for 'the possibility of blessing couples in irregular situations and same-sex couples without officially validating their status or changing in any way the Church's perennial teaching on marriage'.[10] He called for the universal decriminalisation of homosexuality which persists still in many countries. These are signs of hope for the Church that is committed to following in the footsteps of the Christ whose human heart was constantly 'moved with compassion' (Matthew 14:14) and who 'went about doing good' (Acts 10:38).

This issue has in some ways split the Catholic Church because of its stated teaching that God created all humans to be either 'male' or female' and that 'tradition has always declared that homosexual acts are intrinsically disordered, and contrary to the natural law because they close the sexual act to the gift of life and under no circumstances can they be approved'[11]. We examine this teaching and the challenges it presents in Chapter 1.

---

[8] Found at: Pope Francis reminds us of our call to be missionary disciples as stated by the *National Catholic Reporter* (ncronline.org) 6 November, 2024.

[9] Universal Catechism of the Catholic Church, 2357.

[10] *Fiducia Supplicans: On the Pastoral Meaning of Blessings,* Vatican Declaration, 2023.

[11] Universal Catechism of the Catholic Church, 2357.

INTRODUCTION

Catholic Church official teaching remains hesitant, even blind about opening up to embrace LGBTIQA+ people as full human expressions of God's creative love with different but equally blessed sexual attractions and expressions that can be a sharing in God's own Trinitarian Love. In Chapter 1 we explore some of the advances in scriptural scholarship and theology, together with credible science, and a growing evolution of human understanding and knowledge. These new insights make it imperative for the Church to give attention to these developments, with genuine openness of mind and heart.

NOTE: Throughout the Guide, in group sharing, we invite engagement in the processes of Prayerful Conversation, Deep Listening and Open Dialogue so favoured by Pope Francis and now Pope Leo for the future universal Church, and characteristic of both the Australian Plenary Council and the Synod on Synodality.

PRAYERFUL CONVERSATION

You are invited to consider these questions and share your responses to them.

- Are there LGBTIQA+ plus members of my family or social circle?
- How do I relate to them?
- What do I hope to gain by exploring this topic through engagement with the Guide, either individually, or in a group?

THE RAINBOW OF GOD'S CREATION

SHARED PRAYER

Create a new heart in me O Lord.

Open my ears,
my eyes
and my mind

that I may know
and do
Your Will.

Chapter 1

Why has the Church been so slow to change?

The LGBTIQA+ community has been outlawed and persecuted for centuries. A history of fear, entrenched cultural attitudes including religious doctrines and customs, based on 'old' science, together with discredited scriptural and theological interpretations, have left contemporary Catholicism with a major challenge to face.

Criminalisation of homosexuality

It is hard for us to imagine that prior to 1997, Tasmania was dubbed 'Bigots Island' by observers across the globe. South Australia was the first Australian state or territory to decriminalise homosexuality in 1975 and Tasmania was the last in 1997. Each of the states and territories have their own history of struggle towards recognition and safeguarding under the law.[1]

During his papacy, Pope Francis called for the 'decriminalisation' of homosexuality in the remaining 67 countries where LGBTIQA+ people can still be thrown into prison, or even executed, if detected. 'Being homosexual isn't a crime,' the Pope told an Associated Press reporter in 2023, stating that he urged the Bishops in countries where condemnation of gay persons is enshrined in law to be 'converted', and always to 'show tenderness' for them.[2]

Catholic global voices falling on 'hard ground'

Since 2020, new views and questions from Catholics around the world have been brought forward through the broad and deep

> 'Being homosexual isn't a crime,' the Pope told an Associated Press reporter in 2023...'

---

[1] ABC News published a timeline for the decriminalisation of homosexuality, 2015. Found at Timeline: 22 years between first and last Australian states decriminalising male homosexuality, ABC News.

[2] Article, 'Pope says "Being Homosexual isn't a crime"', Nicole Winfield, Jan 26, 2023. Sydney Morning Herald, AAP. Found at: https://www.smh.com.au/world/europe/pope-says-being-homosexual-isnt-a-crime-2023126-p5cfne.html

consultation processes that preceded both the Australian Plenary Council (2020–2021) and the global Synod on Synodality in Rome (2023–2024).

There has been increasing disappointment that submissions have not been seen to be satisfactorily addressed. The response to the final Plenary Council Report from one lay Catholic organisation expressed this disappointment:

> There was a distinct lack of serious attention in the Council agenda and deliberations to the needs of LGBTIQA+ Catholics and divorced Catholics, which remain unaddressed pastoral issues of great importance. The 'weakening' of the original sharing via the submissions remains a disappointment.[3]

During the Continental Phase of the Synod on Synodality, Catholics were invited to identify what local needs and hopes resonated in their context. Among the responses, the need to listen deeply to LGBTIQA+ Catholics and address their full inclusion in the Church was a frequent expression.

It is fair to ask why the Church leadership has been so reluctant to embrace and seriously consider the expressions of support for LGBTIQA+ people in the many thousands of submissions gathered from the six continents. The expressions of hope that the Church would embrace LGBTIQA+ people as full expressions of God's Creation, equal in human dignity with binary Church members seems to be a bridge too far.

Growing urgency and advocacy: what can the church learn from LGBTIQA+ persons?

Advocacy for a better future for LGBTIQA+ people has been developing across the world for more than fifty years. Demonstrations of LGBTIQA+ rights have been mystifying for some people observing from the outside, particularly for those who adhere to strict religious teaching against

---

[3] This response came from a group of parishioners in the Star of the Sea Parish, Burnie Tasmania, where the author was a parishioner involved in group discernments and reporting related to the Plenary Council, 2020/2021.

THE RAINBOW OF GOD'S CREATION

LGBTIQA+ expression. Yet there has been a growing consciousness among many binary people, including Catholics – and especially among the young who have grown up beside LGBTIQA+ people – that they are a gift to both the Church and the world, as is their struggle for full recognition as citizens and children of God. This growing awareness has increasingly inspired advocacy and demonstration in support of their LGBTIQA+ 'siblings'.[4] These 'siblings may be within their immediate biological family or within the wider human community.

Hard questions for Catholic Church leadership to face

And so we ask again: Why has it proved so difficult for authorities in many Christian Churches, including Catholicism, to endorse the experience and claims of the LGBTIQA+ community?

---

[4] The term 'sibling' is used in this guide as a descriptor of the relationship that exists between LGBTIQA+ people and all humans, sharing membership of one human family, created in Love by God. It is the term favoured by coalitions such as Rainbow Catholics Australia and its member groups.

WHY HAS THE CHURCH BEEN SO SLOW TO CHANGE?

The following is an account cited by author Martin Flanagan, of abject failure on the part of a bishop to understand the reality of gay people, including one of his priests. The incident is a sign of the inadequacy of the episcopal formation of those entrusted with the care of the Faithful.

> The priest was attending a meeting in the diocese during the weeks leading up to the Gay Marriage Plebiscite in Australia. The Bishop declared, 'Homosexuals are not part of God's plan.' The priest stood up and responded, 'I'm a gay man, and, as far as I'm concerned, I am part of God's plan, and God loves me.'[5]

Catholics, reflecting on their experience of family or friends who are LGBTIQA+ people, and as citizens of a country that legalised Gay Marriage in 2016, may well ask with increasing urgency, what do those realities mean for their Church?

- What is the Catholic Church called to in light of current legislative and theological developments that are taking account of history, new science and scripture scholarship?

- How can the Church grow in understanding that its religious tradition needs to respond with sincerity and openness to contemporary cultural norms and expectations?

- Why does the Church insist on adhering to its doctrines condemning LGBTIQA+ expressions when scientific evidence and human experience point in another direction towards review and reform?

- Why has the Pope Francis' oft quoted comment 'Who am I to judge?', when asked about the life of a homosexual man, been so celebrated, resonating with people of deep faith, or none?

---

[5] Flanagan M, *The Empty Honour Board: A School Memoir*, Penguin Random House, Australia, 2023, p. 155.

REFLECTION

'... the Church has always had the duty of scrutinizing the signs of the times and of interpreting them in the light of the Gospel. Thus, in language intelligible to each generation, she can respond to the perennial questions which humans ask about this present life and the life to come, and about the relationship of the one to the other. We must therefore recognize and understand the world in which we live, its explanations, its longings, and its often-dramatic characteristics.'

(*Gaudium et Spes*, Pastoral Constitution on the Church in the Modern World, Vatican Council II, 1965, para. 4)

SPIRITUAL CONVERSATION

- How does this quotation from *Gaudium et Spes*, written in 1965, resonate for us in the 21st Century?
- In what ways can LGBTIQA+ realities be seen as a 'sign of the times', in our place and time?
- How do you respond to the challenge Vatican II set out here for the Church?

PRAYER

We pray that we may be open to the gift of Wisdom from the Holy Spirit.

'Come Holy Spirit, fill the hearts of your Faithful and enkindle in them the fire of Your Love. Send forth Your Spirit and they shall be created, and You shall renew the face of the earth.'

'Living in sin?' A very public claim is made

Many of us who are Australians will remember the publicity around the now celebrated case of the Wallaby's Rugby star, Israel Folau, and his public condemnation of homosexuality as contrary of God's law. In 2019, Folau posted on his Instagram account the following message:

> Those that are living in Sin will end up in Hell unless you repent. Jesus Christ loves you and is giving you time to turn away from your sin and come to him.

The message was accompanied by a poster, listing 'Drunks, Homosexuals, Adulterers, Liars, Fornicators, Thieves, Atheists, Idolators' as people for whom 'HELL awaits', needing to 'Repent', and stating, 'Only Jesus Saves'.

The Wallaby team's coach and management, together with Rugby Australia, objected to such a public declaration as discriminatory and a potential breach of the contract issued to team members when they signed up. This was because signing required respect for the code's policies of inclusion and outlawing racist, homophobic, hateful or destructive conduct.

The public position taken by Folau divided the Australian community at the time, when vigorous public debate for and against the legalisation of Gay Marriage preceded the Plebiscite later that year.[6] The majority of Australians supported Gay Marriage, which came into legislation in 2019, but it generated outspoken opposition from faith groups, including from Catholic Church episcopal leadership.[7]

---

[6] ABC News item, 'Israel Folau's posts about 'homosexuals' and 'sinners' draws criticism from rugby union figures and fans', April 11, 2019. Found at: https://www.abc.net.au/news/2019-04-11/israel-filou-slammed-over-latest-anti-gay-comments/10991574

[7] In 2015, the Australian Catholic Bishops Conference issued its booklet, 'Don't Mess with Marriage', to explain its staunch opposition to same sex unions being recognised as 'marriage'. DMM-booklet_web.pdf (sydneycatholic.org)

Need for reconsideration by the Church

This case and others like it, make it urgent for faith communities to examine the cultural influences that have made it possible for historical homophobic beliefs and practice to remain entrenched in their religious beliefs and practices.

In some faiths those now scientifically discredited beliefs remain as powerful influences giving oxygen to discrimination and even forms of persecution against LGBTIQA+ persons.

Folau attributed his stated beliefs that gays are 'sinners' to his devout Christian Faith. Few doubted that he was sincere and convinced in adhering to his beliefs.

It is an exploration of the *nature and origin* of those beliefs that is the subject of this chapter.

Implications for Catholicism

The Church fails at its peril to undertake open and credible examination of the root causes, historically and culturally, that underlie its persistent commitment to Canons and official teachings that condemn LBGTIQA+ identification and expressions.

Many Catholics remain deeply disappointed and some totally disillusioned by the Church's reluctance to act in challenging and renewing its own doctrine and teaching in relation to LGBTIQA+ realities. This reluctance is also surely puzzling for some of the other Christian faiths who have been courageous in facing this challenge, often at great cost. The Catholic Church is recognised as a force for public good in many other areas of human life and destiny, but this issue remains a stumbling block.

A Key Question: We ask, why has condemnation of LGBTIQA+ identity and practice been so consistent throughout much of human history in the Catholic Church, the oldest of the Christian faiths?

Official Catholic Church Teaching

An understanding of the *cultural* factors behind Catholic doctrines and beliefs that still supports condemnation of LGBTIQA+ people and their sexual expression is fundamental.

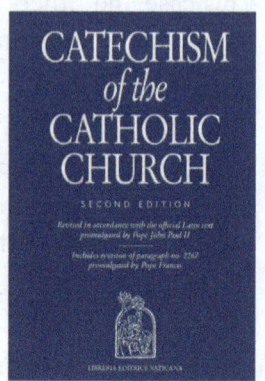

The Catholic Church in its magisterium (official Church teaching) and the Universal Catechism (the formal compendium of Catholic belief) remains explicit in teaching that homosexuality is an 'inclination', which is 'objectively disordered'. The Universal Catholic Catechism states that:

> ... tradition has always declared that 'homosexual acts are intrinsically disordered'. They are contrary to the natural law. They close the sexual act to the gift of life. They do not proceed from a genuine affective and sexual complementarity. Under no circumstances can they be approved.[8]

The Catechism follows that teaching with the conclusion that:

> Homosexual persons are called to chastity. By the virtues of self-mastery that teach them inner freedom, at times by the support of disinterested friendship, by prayer and sacramental grace, they can and should gradually and resolutely approach Christian perfection.[9]

These official doctrines still view homosexuality as a 'disorder' and all homosexual acts as 'sinful'. They are examples of teachings coming from 'above', based on a deductive theology.

In Chapter 4 we examine more synodal and pastoral ways of 'listening with the ear of the heart', a phrase from the Rule of St Benedict[10].

---

[8] The Catechism of the Catholic Church, 2nd Edition, promulgated by Pope John Paul II, 1994, paras. 2357, 2358 and 2359.

[9] The Catechism of the Catholic Church, para. 2358, Rome, 1994.

[10] Rule of S Benedict, Prologue Verse 1-7. Found at: Prologue Verse 1-7, Benedictine Abbey of Christ in the Desert (christdesert.org)

We can become 'disciples of experience', a beautiful phrase that comes from around 1490, from Leonardo da Vinci. He described himself as a 'man without letters' and a 'disciple of experience', explaining, 'Though I have no power to quote from authors, I rely on a far more worthy thing- on experience.'[11] Leonardo was a man comfortable in his own homosexuality.[12]

'Gender ideology'?

The Vatican document *Dignitas Infinita* (March 2024)[13] restates other official Church pronouncements that have invoked the term 'Gender ideology' in reiterating and defending existing Church teaching about LGBTIQA+ realities.[14] 'Gender ideology' is not a helpful term, but rather an expression that can come across as a one hit 'weapon' in the current climate where growing awareness of human diversity is leading to careful study of gender diversity. Catholic parents, priests, pastoral workers, medical practitioners, teachers and others, are seeking sound medical advice and wise counsel about how best to respond to the needs of those to whom they minister who present as 'gender questioning' or 'trans' persons.

The following is an example of pastoral care extended to a secondary school student who seems to be testing the waters in relation to transgender identity.

> A very experienced lead teacher in Mission, Pastoral Care and Religious Education working in an Australian Catholic secondary school shared how his office is 'always open and welcoming for students and they frequently drop in to seek a listening ear and support with their concerns and anxieties.

---

[11] Isaacson, W, *Leonardo Da Vinci*, Simon and Schuster, New York, 2017, p. 69.

[12] Ibid. On p. 69, Isaacson comments that 'Leonardo was romantically and sexually attracted to men and, unlike Michaelangelo, seemed to be just fine with that.' He was moreover a man who had great respect for the evidence and importance of science.

[13] Found at: Declaration of the Dicastery for the Doctrine of the Faith *"Dignitas Infinita"* on Human Dignity (vatican.va) October 2020

[14] The document, 'Male and Female He Created Them: Towards a path of dialogue on the question of gender theory in education', Vatican, 2019, is another example. Found at: Vatican document on gender: Yes to dialogue, no to ideology - Vatican News October 21, 2024.

For example, on one occasion a 'deeply religious' Year 10 student called into the office, explaining in his own way that he wanted to 'educate me about transgender issues'. As the bell was about to ring, I just had time to assure him that he is made in God's image and is loved by God. Over time, he came back and we had some amazing conversations.' [15]

Genuine love and respect towards young people facing and dealing with complex issues like this one, can offer the reassurance that they are not alone and are loved and accepted as the person they are.

In March 2024, research showed that 0.9% of Australians identify as 'gender diverse', and that this group of people have suffered multiple forms of maltreatment as children to a far greater degree than the general population.[16] In response to the study, Bishop Daniel Meagher of Sydney set the tone and issued the challenge for all Catholics, stating:

Clearly, gender diverse people have many challenges to face in life. Community acceptance is undoubtedly one. I hope we can find room in our hearts for compassion, respect and love. We are all children of God, hoping to find happiness and meaning in our lives.[17]

Caution not condemnation

Medical experts remain divided in Australia regarding best medical advice and practice for trans people, especially the young. These specialists have an interest in the findings of the influential 2024

---

[15] Interview with the author, October 5, 2023.

[16] 'Prevalence of Diverse Genders and Sexualities in Australia and Associations with Five Forms of Child Maltreatment and Multi-type Maltreatment.' Joint study, Australian Catholic University and Curtin University, March, 2024. Found at: Research reveals prevalence of gender and sexuality diverse Australians, and finds greater risk of child maltreatment (acu.edu.au).

[17] Rodrigues, M, 'Gender diverse persons need acceptance, love, says bishop following maltreatment study', article in *Catholic Weekly*, Sydney, August 23, 2024. Found at: Loving and improving mental health for gender diverse individuals | The Catholic Weekly Nov 9, 2024.

WHY HAS THE CHURCH BEEN SO SLOW TO CHANGE?

Cass Review in England.[18] Its final report cautioned against hasty or ill-considered administration of medical interventions such as 'puberty blocker' drugs for young gender diverse people.

Parents and educators experience first-hand the vulnerability of young people who may well be persuaded by societal, media or peer pressures during the formative years when they are growing in self-awareness. External influences or lack of their own capacity to judge wisely could lead them to a certitude about their sexual orientation or gender that they may live to review in later years. Prudence and responsible professional guidance is always called for.

However, resorting to blanket condemnation under a 'Gender Ideology' umbrella, leaves the Catholic Church open to the accusation of 'stifling debate'. Respected Cass Report Chair, Dr Hilary Cass, stated in her Final Report:

> Polarisation and stifling of debate do nothing to help the young people caught in the middle of a stormy social discourse, and in the long run will also hamper the research that is essential to finding the best way of supporting them to thrive (p. 13).

The assumption cannot wisely be made that humans who have transitioned or are discerning whether to take that difficult and fraught route, are victims of their own delusion, or taking a choice that is 'sinful', as some parties in the Church claim.

The following example of a young adult transitioning, and other similar examples, can be found within families, schools, parishes and workplaces, giving pause for deep reflection, not blanket condemnation on the part of the Church. The Christian Churches are called to sincerely seek to discern what is just and good, right here, right now, in response to the needs of all humans, including LGBTIQA+ persons.

---

[18] Cass H, Chair, 'Independent review of gender identity services for children and young people: Final report'. Found at: Final Report - Cass Review October 20, 2024.

The urgency to do this well is illustrated in the following account of one family's experience:

> Within a large extended family well-known to us is a family member who, at 24 years of age, has transitioned from female to male, and now uses the pronouns he/him and identifies as male with the name of Mars.
>
> From a young age he struggled to feel comfortable within his own body. This is known as gender dysphoria. In the last few years, Mars has had the privilege to access the appropriate health care, including a gender reassignment surgery and ongoing hormone therapy. Since he started his transition, Mars has had a significant improvement to his sense of self and place in the world. It is crucial for people like Mars and others in the LGBTIQA+ community to have support and acceptance from their family and Church. Parents, siblings and cousins have all supported and respected this decision. In the beginning Mars's Catholic grandmother, like many, found it hard to understand and accept. But the more conversations had, and with more education regarding his transition, she came to realise the importance, not only for his wellbeing, but for her love and support.[19]

The Church's modern teachings have consistently condemned hatred, vilification or forms of disrespect to gay, lesbian or other LGBTIQA+ persons. Church teaching is clear that they are to be afforded pastoral care at all times.[20] However, it must be said, that in Catholic Church teaching they remain officially 'aberrations of nature' and their sexual expressions 'sinful'. These words may well ultimately come to be judged as the height of disrespect and discrimination, as new knowledge in *both the medical sciences*

---

[19] Author interview with the grandmother who provided this account in dialogue with Mars, November, 2024.

[20] The Catechism of the Catholic Church, para. 2358 states, 'The number of men and women who have deep-seated homosexual tendencies is not negligible. This inclination, which is objectively disordered, constitutes for most of them a trial. They must be accepted with respect, compassion, and sensitivity. Every sign of unjust discrimination in their regard should be avoided.

and theology is taken into account and the Church opens itself to thoroughly discern its doctrine and practice in relation to LGBTIQA+ persons. In Chapter 4 we revisit the importance of this discernment process.

How is it so?

We ask, how has Catholicism been influenced and shaped over two millennia in developing its official doctrines related to LGBTIQA+ people? How important and possible is it that these doctrines be reviewed in the light of new knowledge and human experience, uniquely available in this 21st century?

Above: Council of Jerusalem, a conference of the Christian Apostles in Jerusalem, scene of the New Testament, Histoire Biblique de L´Ancien Testament

The first century Church faced up to exclusion

This process of facing the Church's need to deal with new challenges can never be simple or easy. Moral theologian James Keenan SJ explains, 'I do not think that the present anxiety about recognizing the gay Catholic is unlike the 1st century anxiety regarding Gentiles becoming Christians.'[21]

Perhaps then it will take the same openness, prayerful discernment and strong intervention of the Holy Spirit – within a gathering of the Church community similar to the first ecumenical Council of Jerusalem (or a modern Catholic equivalent) – to discern such an important change of attitude, belief and doctrine as this.

As we learn in Acts, Chapter 15, the young Church of the apostles and first disciples was willing to open its membership to the Gentiles (non-Jews) only after *careful communal consideration, discernment and prayer.* Only then were the apostles ready to declare their change of direction in teaching and practice to communities spreading across the known world. The famous insight, 'It seems to the Holy Spirit and to us …' was completed at the first Ecumenical Council at Jerusalem (49 AD in favour of Gentiles being accepted as full members of the Church, without the requirement for circumcision that had been part of the Jewish faith from which Christianity had sprung.

In each of the ecumenical councils since Jerusalem, the Church has been called to discern faith challenges of the time. Many contemporary Catholics long for the day when Catholic Church leadership would adopt that insight from the apostles ('It seems to the Holy Spirit to us that …') and complete it through a contemporary lens to express new doctrine in relation to LGBTIQA+ people. 'It seems to the Holy Spirit, and to us, that LGBTIQA+ people are loving expressions of God's Creation, to be recognised and accepted in the fullness of their distinctive humanity, and in its sexual expression, each one destined to be an *imago dei*, that is, made in the image and likeness of God.'

---

[21] Keenan, J, 'LGBT Catholics and 'disordered' language: A biblical model for change', article, America Magazine, March 12, October 2024. Found at: LGBT Catholics and 'disordered' language: A biblical model for change | America Magazine..

REFLECTION

In the light of Pope Francis' call for the contemporary Catholic Church to be open to all, we can reflect on the apostles' words above as they met in the Council of Jerusalem in the first century. Imagine them wondering whether the Gentiles could be fully accepted into the early Christian community, since they were the 'uncircumcised'. This was their first major challenge as a 'new' Church.

PRAYERFUL CONVERSATION

- Is the Spirit calling you to any new insights in this chapter so far? Share one of them.
- How do you respond to the reality of the young 'trans' person and her 'transition' narrated above? What questions might it raise for you?

THE RAINBOW OF GOD'S CREATION

SHARED PRAYER

*Creator God, may we be open to all people.
You have endowed each of us
with a unique nature and our own life journey.
As we encounter people in daily life,
through family, work or in social settings,
may we learn how genuine respect
and acceptance can characterise
all our relationships.
We ask this in the Spirit of Jesus
who especially welcomed
and loved those who were
outcast or misunderstood
in His time and place.*

WHY HAS THE CHURCH BEEN SO SLOW TO CHANGE?

A history of persecution

It is alarming for us to learn that, throughout history, extreme forms of persecution have been perpetrated against homosexual people, often legitimated by religious doctrine and government ordinances claiming to be designed to guard against public 'immorality', attributed to the presence and actions of these 'unnatural' persons.

One of the worst examples of persecution in the modern era occurred during the mid-20th century when homosexual men, alongside millions of Jews, were rounded up, imprisoned, tortured, and murdered.

During the Nazi era, between 5,000 and 15,000 men were imprisoned in concentration camps as 'homosexual (*homosexuell*) offenders'. This group of prisoners was typically required to wear a pink triangle on their camp uniforms as part of the prisoner classification system.[22]

In the 1980s some gay activists turned the pink triangle upside down and used it as a symbol of liberation; however, it remains as a lingering reminder of terrible persecution.

In seeking to shed some light on the hatred, exclusion and persecution of LGBTIQA+ people, we now consider some of the cultural, theological and scientific factors that have influenced human attitudes and practices over millennia and continue even to the present, with a deep impact on the development of Christian doctrines.

Catholic doctrinal approaches to sex and marriage

In attempting to address questions related to Catholicism and LGBTIQA+ people, the work of English Catholic priest and gay theologian James Alison is a major credible source.

Alison explains that there exists a direct link between Catholic teaching on marriage as a lifelong partnership between a man and a

---

[22] Holocaust Encyclopedia, United States Holocaust Memorial. Found at: Gay Men under the Nazi Regime, Holocaust Encyclopedia (ushmm.org).

Gay and Lesbian Holocaust Memorial in Green Park, Darlinghurst, Sydney (2001) Designed by Russell Rodrigo and Jennifer Gamble to commemorate the gay men and lesbian women who were victims of the Nazis during World War II. Permission granted.

woman, primarily for purposes of procreation, and Catholic teaching against homosexuality.

Alison points out that the modern notion of mutual attraction and *loving fulfilment* being fundamental to marriage and of equal importance to the purpose of *procreation*, is a relatively new sociological concept. Traditionally, in patriarchal societies, marriage was largely a means to create bonds between families and nations, perpetuate dynasties, and ensure the survival of the tribe or people. Individual fulfilment through romantic love and sexual attraction was secondary to these social and political purposes.

Because homosexual unions could never physically produce offspring they were condemned as unnatural and therefore 'disordered' and 'immoral'.

Early Church doctrine informed by primitive science

The early Fathers of the Church were writing theology and refining doctrine during the first 7 centuries of Christianity. They were reliant on the flawed biology of their time which saw women, in Aristotle's phrase, as 'misbegotten males' – passive recipients of, and receptacles for, the male sperm which was believed to be the sole source of new life.[23] The presence and function of the ovary and ovulation were not discovered until the 19th century, and hence a man's sperm was believed to be the source, the 'seed', for the transmission of new life. The ovum as partner bearer of the DNA of life was unknown. Women were deemed to be mere 'receptacles' to receive the all-important sperm, relegated to 'second class status'.

Homosexual men were even less able to be part of procreation than women. They were 'disordered' because their male sexual relations and actions could never conform to this ordained 'order' for the transmission of new life.[24] Biology as a science was rudimentary at best. Not until the 19th century did science begin serious research into the nature of homosexuality.

Modern science opens up new understandings

James Alison traces the development of scientific research in the late 19th century and early 20th century that demonstrated the naturally occurring presence in the human species (and in most other animal species) of a minority group with an intrinsic same-sex attraction. Alison has coined the phrase a 'minority, non-pathological variant' to describe this phenomenon in humans.

---

[23] James Alison visited Australia in 2023. Two events that provide an introduction to his work with LGBTIQA+ and the Catholic Church are cited here. Catalyst for Renewal Forum with James Alison. 'What does radical inclusion really mean for a modern Catholic Church?' Catholic Religious Australia (CRA) Seminar, 'A mission-focused discussion about the Catholic Church and matters LGBTQIA+ with James Alison', 2023. Both an be found at: James Alison Australian Tour Resources – Catholic Religious Australia Oct 4, 2024.

[24] Coloe, Mary, 'A Matter of Justice and Necessity: Women's Participation in the Catholic Church', article found in Compass: a review of topical theology, 45 (3), pp. 13 - 20. This article explains the primitive science underpinning the Church's teaching that women were 'defective' because of the belief that the male sperm was solely responsible for the transmission of life and the woman merely a receptacle of the male seed.

In other words, people who discover they do not have an innate attraction to the opposite sex, are not 'disordered' or 'pathological' but are part of that minority of humans who are *different* from the majority heterosexual population. They 'just are what they are'. The conclusion follows that they are different, but equal in dignity with the majority heterosexual population. For the Christian therefore, they are loving creations of God, no less no more than all of their fellow humans, called to live a virtuous human life, destined to flourish and to find fulfilment, growing in wisdom and grace and free to give of themselves to another in committed human love, just as other humans are.[25]

However the Church has persisted in its doctrine from the time of the Fathers of the Church until now – where all sexual acts outside monogamous marriage between a man and a woman, even faithful same-sex, loving unions free from promiscuity and exploitation of others, remain condemned in Catholic Church doctrine as sinful.

A Catholic safe haven for homosexual men

In order to begin to understand why the Catholic Church fails to face and respond doctrinally and pastorally to LGBTIQA+ issues in the 21st century, we need also to understand that the authority and governance of the Church has been historically in the hands of ordained male clerics.

Those men called to the vocation of priesthood have until recent decades come from societies that condemned all non-heterosexual identification and activity as both illegal and immoral. As we know in some societies such people were persecuted or even killed. At the very least being gay or lesbian was frowned upon and considered abnormal and hence a huge burden to carry.

Over the centuries, the Church has provided a safe haven where those who recognised (or intuited) that they were not heterosexual

---

[25] James Alison, webinar, 'How did we get here? LGBTIQA+ and the Church?', Garratt Publishing, October 2, 2023. Found at: James Alison, How did we get here? LGBTIQA+ and the Church?', YouTube.

in their natural inclination, could serve God and God's people largely free from the threat of being 'discovered' and humiliated or ostracised in wider society. It was understandable that the Church would attract a disproportionate number of gay men into the celibate way of life in the priesthood or a religious order. It is not surprising that pastoral work would attract a number of gay men, as indeed the caring professions are known to do.

A gay parish priest shared an aspect of his own pastoral ministry:

> Rather than *coming out*, I have occasionally practised *inviting in*. When suspecting that a colleague is struggling with sexual orientation, I have asked if it helps them to know my journey. I have found many gay and lesbian laity, religious and clergy in education, counselling and pastoral care who have contributed creatively and generously to the Church and society, but have had to *fly under the radar* because of their sexual orientation and private lives.[26]

Catholic Clerical Culture and Homosexuality

In 2019, extensive research into Catholic clerical life was carried out by French journalist and intellectual Frédéric Martel. Over four years, Martel and his assistant researchers interviewed hundreds of Catholic clerics, cardinals, archbishops, bishops, monsignors, priests and closely associated lay people (e.g. several Swiss Guards were among those who spoke with Martel). The men who were approached and agreed to be interviewed for this research came both from within the Vatican itself and from majority Catholic countries such as Spain, Latin America and Italy. The Roman Curia were in the majority, and the Vatican city itself was at the heart of the study.

---

[26] Confeggi P, *Weaving his world with the Word: Memoir of a Reluctant Cleric*, Huon Design and Print, Tasmania, 2022, p. 60.

Rome seen from St Peter's Basilica

Martel comments that the men interviewed were remarkably 'candid' in sharing their experiences of homosexual 'inclinations' and behaviour among the clergy they knew and worked with on official Church business and in ministry.

Martel's conclusions are reflected in the title of his bestselling book, *In the Closet of the Vatican*.[27] Martel found that there was an entrenched culture of 'Don't ask, don't tell' regarding widespread homosexual practice among the clergy and hierarchy in the Vatican. Similar institutional cover-ups have been found in other traditionally male cultures, for example the military.

Martel's research showed that the cardinals and other clergy most vehemently committed to insisting that the Faithful observe the Church teaching against homosexuality were in many cases themselves closeted and often practicing homosexuals.

The findings are shocking for the average reader but cannot be easily dismissed. Cardinal Timothy Radcliffe OP, chosen by Pope Francis as spiritual guide for the Synod on Synodality, wrote in a review

---

[27] Martel F, *In the Closet of the Vatican: Power, Homosexuality, Hypocrisy*, 2019. Bloomsbury Publishing Plc. London.

of Martel's book, titled *The Carnival is Over*, 'Even if only half of what he claims is true, we are still faced with revelations that are stunning'. He asked, 'How should the Church react?'[28]

It would seem impossible for the Church to face the reality of homosexuality as an accepted part of most modern democracies while the Church still persists in denouncing 'homosexual activity' as a 'moral disorder'.[29] Catholic clerics must act as though they believe and live by Church doctrine while, as Martel's research reveals, astonishing numbers of them have in fact been found to be living double lives in a culture of deceit and cover-up.

It was revealed that some clerics have lived with a faithful single partner within the walls of the Vatican for the major part of their lives as priests, bishops or cardinals. Others have used the services of prostitutes in a well-known network of clubs and establishments in Rome or other cities, sometimes including recent migrants who fled hardship and persecution in their own country. Still others, have groomed and had sexual relationships with seminarians. The evidence is compelling.

Martel did not set out to condemn homosexuality as such; he shares that he is a gay man himself. Rather it is the *hypocrisy* of the clerical culture in Rome and beyond that is his target for exposure.[30] He has found through the testimony of his hundreds of interviews with priests, bishops, cardinals and related lay people that the Catholic Church, while condemning all sexual activity outside monogamous heterosexual marriage, is itself harbouring clerics who are practising homosexuals.

It becomes understandable why Pope Francis had found this one of the most intractable challenges he had faced in cleaning up the Vatican bureaucracy and meeting the pastoral needs of the People of God globally.

---

[28] Radcliffe T, 'The Carnival is Over', article, *The Tablet*, Feb 16, 2019. Found at T-Radcliffe-The-Tablet.pdf (fredericmartel.com)

[29] Joseph Cardinal Ratzinger, Letter to the Bishops of the Catholic Church on the Pastoral Care of Homosexual Persons, Congregation for the Doctrine of the Faith Rome, 1896, p. 7.

[30] Op cit p. xiii.

It is understandable too that the all-male Church clerical governance may find it too close for comfort to seriously open discussion around LGBTIQA+ issues when its own culture has elements of 'don't see, don't tell' that daily risk exposure.

Having women and married men admitted to priestly Ordination, as many of the laity have requested, would create an immediate risk of exposure and challenge to the clerical status quo. Maintaining secrecy places an obstacle to what James Alison refers to as 'talkability'; that is, open conversation and respectful listening that could lead to action and reform of Catholic Church attitudes and teaching about LGBTIQA+ people and their ways of living and loving.[31]

Civil law can lead the way

Many Catholic families have LGBTIQA+ children who are protected from discrimination and bullying under civil law. Australian Catholics like all citizens must honour the laws of their country that now recognise the dignity and rights of LGBTIQA+ citizens to live and love in peace as they wish.

Secular society in a democracy like Australia where law is founded upon The Universal Declaration of Human Rights, can be in a position to inform and influence Church teaching that is not yet in conformity with its own Catholic Social Teachings. These modern teachings are founded in principles that include Equality, Justice for all, Human Dignity and Participation. The Church needs to get its own house in order to be a clear 'light to the nations' rather than an alienating organisation for so many Catholics who support the rights of LGBTIQA+ people in society as well as in the Church.

The Australian feedback from the more than 270,000 submissions that flooded in to the Plenary Council in 2019, together with the global consultations from the six continents in preparation for the 2023/24 Synod referred to above, revealed that many Catholics want their Church to give public recognition to the dignity and rights

---

[31] This concept ('talkability') used in this context by James Alison is explored in an address to Catalyst for Renewal, Sydney, 27 Sept, 2023. Found at: What does radical inclusion really mean for a modern synodal Church, James Alison Theology

of LGBTIQA+ people through revision of Church Canon Law and consequently of the Universal Catechism.

Chapter 2 considers these processes of consultation in more detail.

Biblical mis-interpretation

Israel Folau, in his condemnation of homosexuality referred to earlier, relied on the Bible for authority, citing particularly Leviticus 18 and Leviticus 20. These texts are two of the so-called 'Clobber' texts, that is, biblical texts that are used to condemn ('clobber') homosexuality.[32] The texts most frequently cited as clear biblical teaching against homosexuality include:

- **Genesis 1 and 2**
  The creation by God of male and female humans as companions for one another and the command to 'Increase and multiply' through procreation.

- **Genesis 19-38**
  The wickedness of Sodom and Lot's hospitality towards and protection of the two 'men' (angels), threatened with rape by the men of Sodom. They in turn lead Lot and his family to safety.

- **Leviticus 18:22**
  'Do not have sexual relations with a man as one does with a woman; that is detestable.'

- **Romans 1:25-27**
  Paul refers to '… shameful lusts. Even their women exchanged natural sexual relations for unnatural ones. In the same way the men also abandoned natural relations with women and were inflamed with lust for one another. Men committed shameful acts with other men, and received in themselves the due penalty for their error'.

---

[32] A useful descriptor for these texts is found at 'UnClobbering the Bible: A Fresh Perspective on Inclusion', Ministry Forum, the Website for Ministry Forum: The Centre for Lifelong Learning at Knox College, University of Toronto. 6th October, 2024.

- **1 Corinth 6:9-11**
  ... Be not deceived: neither the sexually immoral nor idolaters nor adulterers nor men who have sex with men[a] nor thieves nor the greedy nor drunkards nor slanderers nor swindlers will inherit the kingdom of God...

- **1 Timothy 1:9-11**
  The 'Law' is made 'for the sexually immoral, for those practicing homosexuality ...'

- **Jude 6-7**
  Sodom and Gomorrah committed sexual sins and pursued homosexual activities, serving 'as an example of those who suffer the punishment of eternal fire'.

How can we authentically interpret the Bible?

World renowned Old Testament scholar, Methodist Pastor Walter Brueggemann, commented on these 'clobber' texts within the total context of the Bible in a way that can guide the reader in their interpretation. Firstly, Brueggemann stated that texts like those in Leviticus Chapter 18 and 20 cannot be simply 'explained away'. Nor can those explicit texts in Paul, Timothy and Jude. However, they are not to be read without taking into account *the whole story* of God's Word revealed in the totality of the Bible, and most importantly, in the life and teaching of Jesus, recorded in the Gospels.

Brueggemann explained that these 'clobber' texts sit within what he refers to as the 'rigor' stream of scripture (or the 'Torah', the legalistic tradition), while other sacred texts like Isaiah sit within the 'welcome' stream of the Bible (or the 'Prophetic' and 'Wisdom' traditions). In the end, Brueggemann insisted it is the Gospel, with Jesus' openness to the 'other', the 'stranger', the 'wounded' and the 'lost', that must triumph over legalism and the 'Law' as expounded in Leviticus and other parts of the Bible. The Law in Leviticus set out moral codes suited to ancient times and tribal cultures. The Israelites were living in the midst of Canaanites and other 'enemies' and 'foreigners' whose ways of living threatened to morally 'contaminate' them. As an amusing verse of our childhood somewhat crudely expressed it:

> A curious race were the Persians
> They had such peculiar diversions
> They used up the day in the ordinary way
> And saved up the nights for perversions

Jewish Scripture scholar Amy-Jill Levine has extensively examined the 'clobber texts' and concludes that the moral laws found in Leviticus and emanating from a pre-Christian patriarchal era, intended for Stone Age desert cultures, cannot be expected to be credible moral guides in contemporary human cultures.[33]

Brueggemann made clear that any reading of scripture is undertaken within a particular context, time and place, and each reader brings a unique lens of interpretation to bear on the text. Hence, their reading, even unconsciously, reflects the reader's own particular biases and needs. Brueggemann made several further important points in interpreting scripture: *human experience* is always to be respected, we are called to be open as Christians to *'embrace God's newness'*, we are 'geared towards *justice and mercy'*, and our faith calls us to the *'embrace of the other'*. And so Brueggemann concluded that, 'because our hope is in the God of the

> *'Because our hope is in the God of the Gospel and in no other, the full acceptance of LGBTQ persons follows as a clear mandate of the Gospel in our time.'*
>
> Walter Brueggemann

---

[33] The Biblical scholarship of Levine has much to offer in this context. In particular her article, 'How to read the Bible's "clobber passages" on homosexuality, found at: Amy-Jill Levine: How to read the Bible's "clobber passages" on homosexuality, Outreach.

Gospel and in no other, the full acceptance of LGBTIQA+ persons follows as a clear mandate of the Gospel in our time.'[34]

The Catholic Church has continued to be resistant to accepting the full doctrinal and pastoral implications of best scriptural scholarship in relation to the passages in the Bible cited above. These passages continue to be relied upon in support of official Church teaching condemning homosexuality as an 'objective disorder' and homosexual acts as 'intrinsically evil'. For example, the 1986 'Letter to the Bishops of the Catholic Church on the Pastoral Care of Homosexual Persons', issued by then Cardinal Joseph Ratzinger, draws on them all.[35]

Fear of Church disunity and potential schism

Catholic theologian and gay priest James Alison, already quoted, is a highly respected scholar and pastor. He offers a lifetime of study in bringing together scriptural, scientific and historical research to show the flaws in Catholic teaching about LGBTIQA+ people and related issues. Alison's life's work as a theologian positively demonstrates that LGBTIQA+ people are the expressions of God's loving creation as are the other members of the human family, with the same rights to flourish and express their human, sexual love.

However, Alison has also stated he understands that a sudden doctrinal change toward full acceptance of LGBTIQA+ people could pose a serious threat to the unity of the Catholic Church, deeply divided as it is over this issue. After the promulgation of the Vatican document *Fiducia Supplicans*,[36] which both affirms the Church's traditional teaching about marriage while allowing the 'blessing' of other faithful loving unions (including homosexual union), Alison stated that Catholics need to appreciate the Pope's position of

---

[34] Brueggemann W, 'How to read the Bible on homosexuality', article, September 4, 2022. Found a: O2utreach website: https://outreach.faith

[35] Found at: Letter to the Bishops of the Catholic Church on the Pastoral Care of Homosexual Persons (vatican.va). October 1, 2024.

[36] Declaration, *Fiducia Supplicans*: On the pastoral meaning of blessings. Cardinal Victor Fernandes, Vatican Dicastery for the Doctrine of the Faith, Dec. 2023. Found at: https://www.vatican.va/roman_curia/congregations/cfaith/documents/rc_ddf_doc_20231218_fiducia-supplicans_en.html October 1, 2024.

responsibility to avoid schism. Alison cautions, 'Let us remember that there is no major Christian body that has been able to deal with this matter without the threat, or actuality, of schism.'[37] We await the approach the Church will take in this regard under the leadership of Pope Leo XIV.

This threat can be seen as a strong factor influencing the slow pace of the Church in addressing LGBTIQA+ issues and concerns, but cannot be used as an excuse for failure to address them in a timely and thorough manner. Pope Francis wisely tried to balance pull and push, pressure for and against, radical change in traditional teaching within a truly global organisation made up of diverse cultures and worldviews. LGBTIQA+ has proved to be one of the most challenging areas for open discussion at the Synod on the Family (2015), the Synod on Young People (2018) and the latest on Synodality (2013/24), as well as in other Church settings.

Even the use of the accepted nomenclature (varyingly as LGBTQIA+; LGBTQ; LGBT) has been considered too divisive for inclusion in both the Australian Plenary Council Final Report and the Summary Report from the first session of the Synod on Synodality. That has been a cause of both pain and anger for some Catholics who have spent a lifetime waiting for change.

A stumbling block

From all six continents there have been strong Catholic voices, both individual and communal, calling for open discussion and deep reflection on LGBTIQA+ realities.

> One Australian episcopal voice has courageously and consistently committed to lead the Church as a 'house for all peoples, a Church where there is less an experience of exclusion but more an encounter of radical love, inclusiveness and solidarity, irrespective of sexual orientation, marital status and situation'. And further this voice has stated,

---

[37] Alison J, article 'LGBT, the Church and the new rules of the game', *The Tablet*, Jan. 2024. Found at: LGBT, the Church and the new rules of the game, James Alison Theology, October 1, 2024.

'We must commit ourselves to the task of reaching out to our LGBTI brothers and sisters, affirming their dignity and accompanying them on our common journey towards the fullness of life and love in God.'[38]

Some Catholics dissent from and are highly critical of a bishop who is prepared to publicly encourage openness to change in the Catholic Church, even with a radical Gospel call such as this.

Australian Bishop Geoffrey Robinson (1937-2020), eminent scripture scholar and beloved pastor and guide for the Church in Sydney, studied extensively the moral issues related to human sexuality. He questioned the Church's teaching that every human sexual act must be both 'procreative' (open to the possibility of the transmission of new life) and 'unitive' (an expression of genuine love), within a heterosexual marriage. Robinson offers powerful lines of thought critiquing both the Church's historical reliance on the concept of 'Natural Law' as a basis for its theology, and its undervaluing of human experience, both which risk placing limitations on the limitless Love of God. In defence of loving, monogamous, faithful expressions of love between two humans, including those incapable of transmitting life (infertile or same sex couples), his powerful conclusion is:

> It was God who created a world in which there are both heterosexuals and homosexuals. This is not a mistake on God's part that human beings are meant to repair; it is simply an undeniable part of God's creation.[39]

Conversion Therapy

In some secular and Catholic settings, Conversion Therapy is still believed to be an acceptable way to 'treat' individuals whose

---

[38] Words from Bishop Vincent Long, extracted from his Installation Homily and his Letter to the Diocese on the occasion of the Gay Marriage Plebiscite. Cited in Confeggi P, *Weaving his world with the Word: Memoir of a Reluctant Cleric*, Huon Design and Print, Tasmania, 2022, p. 60.

[39] Robinson, G, 'Towards a new understanding of LGBT lives and love,' given at an International Conference towards pastoral care with homosexual and trans people (Rome, Italy, October 3, 2014). Found at: Bishop Geoffrey Robinson: "Towards a new understanding of LGBT lives and love", Ways of Love (wordpress.com).

orientation is other than heterosexual. Conversion Therapy invites LGBTIQA+ people to turn away from what they believe to be their intrinsic sexual orientation and become heterosexual in orientation, still seen by some as the only 'normal' expression.[40]

If that is not possible for a Catholic person, they are then called to lead a fully 'chaste' life,[41] that is, a life given completely to the Love of God and the service of others. We might say 'a life similar to that of vowed religious', because they are required to surrender willingly the joy and fulfilment of loving sexual experience that is physically attractive and potentially fulfilling for them.

Catholics and others who have 'been through' a process of therapy aimed at 'Conversion' or 'healing' in relation to their same sex attraction have shared that it has not brought a positive outcome for their lives as was promised. As one survivor of the therapy explained, 'The problem is that there's still this undercurrent that [same-sex attraction] is a problem to be rid of, and that I'm not whole, healthy, good, complete as long as I still have it.'[42] It is offering a 'cure to a non-existent illness'.

The practice of Conversion Therapy has been condemned as harmful to human development by medical science and as such is being progressively banned by state and territory governments around Australia, already criminalised in New South Wales (2024), the Australian Capital Territory, Victoria and under consideration in South Australia and Tasmania. In discerning its own responses, the Church needs to open itself to both the human experience of its

---

[40] The Merriman Webster Dictionary definition of Conversion Therapy is: 'the use of any of various methods (such as aversive stimulation or religious counselling) in an attempt to change a person's sexual orientation to heterosexual or to change a person's gender identity to correspond to the sex the person was identified as having at birth', found at: Conversion therapy Definition & Meaning, *Merriam-Webster*, Oct. 30, 2024.

[41] Op cit., *The Catechism of the Catholic Church*, para 2359 states, 'Homosexual persons are called to chastity. By the virtues of self-mastery that teach them inner freedom, at times by the support of disinterested friendship, by prayer and sacramental grace, they can and should gradually and resolutely approach Christian perfection.'

[42] Tushnet E, Article, 'Conversion therapy is still happening in Catholic spaces - and its effects on LGBT people can be devastating', America: The Jesuit Review, May 13, 2021. Found at: Conversion therapy is still happening in Catholic spaces–and its effects on LGBT people can be devastating, *America Magazine*. October 30, 2024.

LGBTIQA+ members and the findings of credible health, medical and social sciences.

Courage International

'Courage International' is a Catholic organisation that was founded in 1978 in New York to pastorally care for people of same-sex attraction, while offering them spiritual guidance in living out the teaching of the Church requiring chastity as their life's 'sacrificial offering' to God.[43] The organisation comes under some scrutiny because of its close resemblance to Conversion Therapy in a Catholic context.

There are stumbling blocks hindering the timely review of the Church's teachings. They are a source of frustration to reform-minded Catholics who see their Church losing credibility in societies that increasingly recognise LGBTIQA+ people as a 'normal' though minority version of the human family.

Many young people see no relevance for a Church that does not embrace their LGBTIQA+ siblings, friends and colleagues and their sexual orientation as equal in dignity with heterosexuals. This is a tragic loss for Catholicism. Many Catholics and their families have abandoned the church, believing they would flourish better outside it. Those who remain need 'Good Shepherds' who are prepared to 'go the extra mile', lovingly tending to them.

'Stones' of harsh doctrine

Prior to the opening of the second session of the Synod on Synodality in October 2024, a solemn ritual of Reconciliation was held for members of the Synod, led by Pope Francis. Argentinian Cardinal Victor Fernandez, Prefect of the Dicastery for the Doctrine of the Faith, read aloud the following words from a prayer composed by Pope Francis, expressing, 'shame for all the times that in the church, especially us pastors who are entrusted with the task of confirming

---

[43] Found at: Timeline - Courage International, Inc. (couragerc.org)

our brothers and sisters in the faith, have not been able to guard and propose the Gospel as a living source of eternal newness, (instead) 'indoctrinating it' and risking reducing it to a pile of dead stones to be thrown at others.'[44]

For many LGBTIQA+ Catholics, their families and allies, the Church's doctrinal expressions and pastoral exclusions have deeply wounded their self-respect and created often insurmountable barriers to their human fulfilment.

Surely the Church must seek out and find a way to turn those 'stones' into food for the spiritual journey and reach out its arms to embrace those who are still excluded.

The following is an account of a young man who 'came out' feeling 'stoned' by the Church's stance towards him, and rejected by his family:

> When Danny came out to his family, they sent him to talk with their parish priest who told him to pray harder and go to therapy. He was sent to a Christian psychologist and prescribed electro shock treatment. After numerous sessions with no apparent changes, he sank further into depression, with thoughts of suicide. He was at his wit's end. His youth group leader in whom he confided, had confirmed that unless he changed, he would remain outside God's love and go to hell. The last straw was when he was told he should no longer serve at the altar nor lead the music ministry because he might influence others and bring shame on their church. He decided to leave both the church and his family.[45]

---

[44] Found at: Pope to Synod: Church Must Recognise, Ask Pardon for its Sins - The Southern Cross (scross.co.za)

[45] This testimony was shared during a Ritual of Lament celebrated on August 13, 2016 at St Joseph's Catholic Church, Newtown, Australia. It was sponsored by Rainbow Catholics Inter-Agency for Ministry, Australia, and Newtown Catholic Parish and Acceptance Sydney, with assistance from Uniting Church Minister Rev. Dorothy McRae McMahon, Waterloo, Sydney. Found at: Order_of_Service_for_Lament_and_Apology_Liturgy_to_LGBTIQ_8.16.pdf (ampjp.org.au) October 17, 2024.

REFLECTION

Reading from the Letter to the Romans

What, then, shall we say in response to these things? If God is for us, who can be against us?...Who then is the one who condemns? No one. Christ Jesus who died—more than that, who was raised to life—is at the right hand of God and is also interceding for us. Who shall separate us from the love of Christ? Shall trouble or hardship or persecution or famine or nakedness or danger or sword?...No, in all these things we are more than conquerors through him who loved us...neither height, nor depth, nor anything else in all creation, will be able to separate us from the love of God in Christ Jesus our Lord.[46] (Romans 8:31, 34–35, 37, 39)

Sit in prayerful silence meditating on this passage.

---

46 Taken from the Ritual referred to in Footnote 28.

PRAYFUL CONVERSATION

- How do you respond to the account above of the young gay man who was rejected within his Catholic community?
- Share a phrase or sentence from the Reading from Romans that you feel may have comforted that young man.

PRAYER

*Spend some moments
in quiet prayer
in response to what
you have heard just now.*

Conclusion

Signs of hope

In the next chapter we examine some signs of hope and winds of change blowing through the Catholic Church; signs that promise a better future for the Church to be fully open to, and inclusive of all God's human family.

Pope Francis expressed the call for inclusion of all, with his now famous shout-out, *'Todos, todos, todos'* ('Everyone, everyone, everyone') at World Youth Day in Lisbon, 2023[47]. The Pope was setting the tone and the benchmark for a constantly renewed Church, open to all without exception.

This theme of inclusion is more than a popular catchcry to appeal to a young audience at World Youth Days. It is the theme of the New Testament expressed in St Paul's Letter to the Galatians – we are told that in 'Christ Jesus' there is no longer division between 'Jew and Greek', 'male and female', 'slave and free'. These are representations of the categories of separateness in Paul's ancient world. Yet, he concludes, 'We are all one in Christ Jesus.' (Galatians 3:28). By extension we could add to Paul's list of contrasting categories, 'LGBTIQA+ people and binary people', in recognising the cultural context of today.

---

[47] White C, *Catholic Reporter*, 'Pope doubles down on message that church is open to all, including LGBTQ people and women', article, Aug. 6, 2023. Found at: Pope doubles down on message that church is open to all, including LGBTQ people and women, *National Catholic Reporter* (ncronline.org), October 16, 2024.

Chapter 2

The tide is turning: *Signs of Catholic support for LGBTIQA+ people*

There have been positive steps in Catholicism from Pope Francis, from the work of LGBTIQA+ Catholics and their allies, from dialogue with other churches, and from the People of God speaking and listening through the Plenary Council and the Synod on Synodality.

In this chapter we explore some very positive signs within the Catholic Church, with evidence of movement forward in many countries in solidarity with LGBTIQA+ Catholics and their challenges. There is a dawning understanding of the need for reform of the Church's dismal track record in relating to LGBTIQA+ realities and lives.

A Pope who embraces LGBTIQA+ people

Who am I to judge?

One of the most often quoted of Pope Francis' many responses to journalists during his legendary off-the-cuff media interviews on flights back to Rome, came early in his papacy.

After returning from Brazil in 2013, the Pope was asked about the dilemma of a reportedly gay priest being appointed to the Vatican. He replied, 'If they accept the Lord and have good will, who am I to judge them?' That part of the question, 'Who am I to judge?' has become a signature quotation from Francis and a sign to the world that the traditional approaches of condemnation and alienation will no longer serve.[1]

Dialogue with gay and transgender people

Pope Francis met on several occasions with gay and transgender people, affirming their innate dignity as God's creation and listening deeply to their stories.

> In 2015, a fervently Catholic Spanish transgender man wrote to the Pope and told him he had been marginalised and rejected in his parish. He requested a meeting with His Holiness to explain transgender issues and receive the Pope's blessing. Francis not only phoned the man but paid for him to come to Rome, personally reassuring him, 'You are a son of God and the Church loves you and accepts you as you are.'[2]

---

[1] McElwee, J, 'Who am I to Judge?' article, National Catholic Reporter, Jan 10, 2016.

[2] Fox, Thomas C,, 'Pope Francis meets with, hugs transgender man', article, National Catholic Reporter, Jan 13, 2015. Found at: Report: Pope Francis meets with, hugs transgender man | National Catholic Reporter (ncronline.org) October 8, 2023.

This is not an isolated case.

In 2019 Stephen K Amos, a prominent face on British television, was part of the BBC2 show, *Pilgrimage: The Road to Rome*. Amos was one of eight celebrities travelling a section of Via Francigena, the Pilgrimage path from Canterbury to Rome. As they approached the Eternal City, an opportunity arose to meet with Pope Francis. Amos refused, stating that as a gay man he did not feel comfortable, that is, unless they could be free to ask any questions they had for the Pope. The response came back from Francis that he would be open to anything the group might like to put to him. During their meeting, Amos told the Pope, 'So me coming on this pilgrimage, being non-religious, I was looking for answers and faith. But as a gay man, I don't feel accepted.' The Pope responded,

> 'Giving more importance to the adjective (gay) rather than the noun (man), this is not good. We are all human beings and have dignity. It does not matter who you are or how you live your life, you do not lose your dignity. There are people who prefer to select or discard people because of the adjective – these people don't have a human heart.'[3]

In response to the experience of meeting with Pope Francis, Amos explained:

> 'He didn't shut anybody down, he was very clear in what we said about all being God's children, all the things you don't normally hear. So, I was in full respect of the man. I had already planned what I would do if he had said something I didn't agree with or that would add more shame on people's lives. I would have respectfully excused myself. I couldn't live with myself otherwise.'

The Pope went on to say at the end of the encounter with the eight pilgrims, 'For those of you who are believers, pray for me. For those of you who do not believe, could you wish me a good journey, so I do not let anyone down.'

---

[3] Podcast. Charles Collins, 'Pope Francis tells gay man "you do not lose your dignity", on BBC show, April 19, 2019. Found at: Pope Francis tells gay man 'you do not lose your dignity' on BBC show | Crux (cruxnow.com) October 12 2024.

Pope Francis congratulates Acceptance Australia

In 2023, Sr Jeannine Gramick – co-founder in the USA of the Catholic support organisation for LGBTIQA+ Catholics, New Ways Ministry – met with Pope Francis and informed him that the Australian gay Catholic support organisation Acceptance, was celebrating 50 years of ministry since its foundation in 1973.[4] As a result the Pope sent a message of recognition and congratulation to Acceptance. Its media release announcing the Pope's good wishes read:

> Pope Francis' greetings were both a surprise and a delight to Acceptance members, their families and supporters across Australia. None of us expected such a greeting, but Pope Francis is such a wonderful Pope, why were we surprised? His welcoming, pastoral and caring interaction with LGBTQ+ people, extending back to his time as Archbishop and Cardinal in Argentina, is a powerful signpost and his greetings on our 50th anniversary reinforces his genuine concern for those marginalised in the Church

Positive encounters with LGBTIQA+ people were a feature of Pope Francis' papacy. Although there has been no change in official Church teaching, the symbolism and witness of these encounters certainly paves the way for a new openness and willingness to learn on the part of the Pope and the Church.

---

[4] Found at: Pope Francis congratulates Acceptance on its 50th anniversary - Acceptance (gaycatholic.com.au)

REFLECTION

A Reading About Pilgrimage

Catholics, including their Pope, are part of the Pilgrim People of God, as taught in *Lumen Gentium*, Article 6: 'The Church, while on earth it journeys in a foreign land away from the Lord, is like in exile.' Echoing Vatican II, this sense of Church as pilgrim is also central to Pope Francis. In *Evangelii Gaudium*, he insists that the Church is 'first and foremost a people advancing on its pilgrim way towards God.' In a 2021 address, Pope Francis said, 'When the Church stops, she is no longer Church, but a beautiful pious association which imprisons the Holy Spirit.' Journeying is part of our nature as Christians – Church is not a 'what', it is who we are. We are pilgrim. Being pilgrim means to be not at home; to be vulnerable, but also enriched by the journey.[5]

---

[5] Pizzy, Antonia, based on article, 'The Pilgrim Church', *Outlook*, Parramatta Diocese, Spring Edition, 2022. Found at: The Pilgrim Church, Catholic Outlook October 12, 2024.

SPIRITUAL CONVERSATION

- How did the story in this chapter of the eight British Pilgrims visiting Rome resonate with you?
- In what sense can the Catholic Church be seen as 'on pilgrimage' in relation to LGBTIQA+ people and their realities?

SHARED PRAYER

*Open our eyes and ears Lord
that we may see your face in all people,
fellow travellers on life's journey
regardless of race, gender, age,
cultural background or faith orientation.
May we love all that You have made
as signs of Your Love.*

World Youth Day

At World Youth Day in Lisbon 2023, the Pope gave this message of radical inclusion to the 1.5 million young people present:

> Please, let us not convert the church into a customs office, where only the 'just', 'good', and 'properly married' can enter while leaving everyone else outside. No. The church is not that; rather it is a place for 'righteous and sinners, good and bad, everyone, everyone, everyone.'

LGBTIQA+ youth representatives

Among the vast crowd – wearing rainbow sashes – was a small but visible representation of LGBTIQA+ youth sponsored by the Catholic organisation Dignity USA. A spokesperson for the group stated, 'Our purpose for being at World Youth Day was to be a visible, affirming, and encouraging presence for LGBTQ Catholics and allies from around the world.[6] Many people came up to speak with them, including Archbishop Anthony Fisher of Sydney. A reporter for the group, Cassidy Klein, said she believes the archbishop 'wanted to learn from them about how best to engage with LGBTQ+ people in the church'.

We can hope this occurred in the grace of that moment of encounter. This public presence and witness of LGBTIQA+ young people was a first at World Youth Day and a brave step for the group. Their presence, supported by Fr James Alison, was not without expressions of objection and insults being directed at them.[7] For Cassidy Klein, it was a life-changing experience, for himself and for the future Church: He added:

> My World Youth Day experience reminded me why I love being Catholic – why this identity, even though it's complicated, means so much to me. I want to continue to commit to be visible in church spaces, carrying the bravery of Catholics throughout time, all over the world, who are witnesses to a different way, to a more loving church.

---

[6] 'LGBTQ+ Pilgrims to World Youth Day Were (a) Visible, Affirming Presence,' An article from New Ways Ministry Website. Found at: LGBTQ+ Pilgrims to World Youth Day Were Visible, Affirming Presence - New Ways Ministry October 6, 2024.

[7] Alessandro Previti. Article, 'The Fight for Inclusion: LGBTIQA+ Christians at World Youth Day 2023.' Found at: Search results for 'World youth day 2023', Global Network of Rainbow Catholics, October 7, 2024

> **There is space in the Church for Everyone, Everyone, Everyone**
>
> (Todos, Todos, Todos)
>
> Pope Francis World Youth Day 2023

REFLECTION

A reading from the Letter of St Paul to the Galatians 3:26–29

So in Christ Jesus you are all children of God through faith, for all of you who were baptized into Christ have clothed yourselves with Christ. There is neither Jew nor Gentile, neither slave nor free, nor is there male and female, for you are all one in Christ Jesus. If you belong to Christ, then you are Abraham's seed, and heirs according to the promise.

Spend some moments silently reflecting on this scripture passage.

PRAYERFUL CONVERSATION

- How do you respond to Paul's teaching here?
- In what sense are Christians called to 'Inclusion' for all?
- Share some of your hopes for a genuinely inclusive Church.

THE RAINBOW OF GOD'S CREATION

PRAYER

*Share spontaneous prayers of thanks
from the heart
for the gifts of Creation
given by God in Love
and extending to all.*

Organisations in Support of LGBTIQA+ Catholics

One of the lesser-known ministries of the Catholic Church is ministry to LGBTIQA+ people. In several countries Catholic support groups have been in existence for over fifty years. In this chapter we introduce some of them, their purpose and their achievements.

A safe parish to gather for prayer, study, community and Eucharist

For many years Sydney Priest Fr Peter Maher celebrated the Eucharist in the inner-city Sydney parish of St Jospeh's Newtown, where many LGBTIQA+ Catholics and others found a spiritual home. Here they knew they were among friends, able to relax and be themselves with full recognition, respect and love afforded to them. When Fr Peter died of cancer in 2022, the full extent of his ministry became more widely understood as tributes poured in. The LGBTIQA+ people with whom he shared Catholic life and the love of Christ deeply mourned and missed him as a brother. He was one of those Catholic priests who seek out the 'lost', including LGBTIQA+ people who often feel ostracised in their family, and/or parish, workplace or school community. It was as natural as air for Peter to see every one of them as children of God, made in God's image and called to live a dignified life as followers of Christ, comfortable in their own skin.

The following are some examples of Australian Catholic organisations founded to support and be a voice for LGBTIQA+ Catholics and others.

National Catholic organisation *Acceptance*

Acceptance, existing in several states of Australis – referred to earlier in this chapter – is one of the oldest Catholic organisations of its kind in the world. The *Acceptance Perth LGBTIQA+ Catholics* website reads:

> Acceptance Perth LGBT Catholics is a fully inclusive and affirming group comprising of LGBTIQA+ Catholics, their families, and their friends. We offer a place for hope, healing, and peace for those seeking a community where LGBTIQA+ people of faith can be their true selves and live out their faith with full flourishing of their humanity. By gathering together, embracing the truth about ourselves, and celebrating God's love, we seek to point towards the full inclusivity to which God is calling us.[8]

It is interesting to note that although there was no officially appointed LGBTIQA+ person as a representative at the Synod on Synodality 2023/24, Acceptance Perth records the presence of one of its members at a much earlier diocesan Assembly in the 1980's.

> In 1989, Jim Seiler attended the Perth Archdiocesan Assembly as the official delegate to represent the Catholic gay community. This was seen by many as some formal recognition for the role of Acceptance in the diocese. Approximately 600 delegates

---

[8] Found at: https://www.acceptanceperth.com/about-us/ Oct. 10, 2024

attended this event, and the ministry of homosexual people was mentioned a number of times.[9]

It is hard to imagine what a breakthrough within Catholic life in Perth this must have been at the time. One can only speculate how different the Church's relationship with LGBTIQA+ people could have been if this openness had continued and strengthened during the past 35 years.

In 2019, Angela Han, a Perth-based Catholic bisexual woman, was inspired to revive *Acceptance Perth LGBTIQA+ Catholics*, twenty-six years after it had ceased in 1993. This decision was triggered by her attendance at World Youth Day in Poland and her own need to find a true home where she could be free to be her authentic self in her Church.

At this point we share a prayer which Angela Han prayed with thousands of people online at a national webinar she facilitated in 2023.[10]

Angela Han, Acceptance Perth LGBTIQA+ Catholics

---

[9] Ibid.

[10] The webinar was entitled 'JAMES ALISON: How did we get here: LGBTIQA+ and the Church?' and it was co-sponsored by Australasian Catholic Coalition for Church Reform (ACCCR), Rainbow Catholics InterAgency for Ministry, Garratt Publishing, Yarra Theological Union (YTU), and Catholic Religious Australia (CRA). It signalled the growing support for LGBTIQA+ among Catholic organisations. The webinar can be found at: https://www.garrattpublishing.com.au/blog/post/james-alison-lgbtiqa-and-the-church/ Oct 10, 2023.

PRAYER FROM ANGELA

Lord God our Maker
The work of your hands reveals
boundless goodness and glory
From intricate snowflakes to majestic peaks
And every sunrise
Your infinite love shapes our world and each of us.
As we gaze upon your diverse children
may we always appreciate
the diversity of each person,
regardless of their identity:
straight, lesbian, gay, bisexual,
transgender, queer, bisexual, intersex, asexual.
We celebrate the unique artistry
you've woven into each heart
Your love creates us all.
Forgive our shortcomings Lord.
For failing to see the beauty in others,
for our apathy, and for our silence
When we should have spoken.
Your love forgives us all.
We pray for unity, tenderness, justice
and compassion, that
The world may know you through our
love for one another.
Your love heals us all.

> **PRAYERFUL CONVERSATION**
> - Share any experience of any gender diverse person/s you have encountered.
> - In what ways has your understanding changed through encounter and conversation?

Rainbow Catholics InterAgency for Ministry – Australia (RCiA)

The word 'Ministry' is significant in the description this Catholic organisation offers for both the curious and the profoundly interested:

> Our Ministry: We are a pastoral interagency supporting pastoral workers, pastoral leaders and pastoral organisers in the Australian Catholic church.
>
> Affirmed by our Christian faith and supported by Catholic Social Teaching, the primary purpose of the Rainbow Catholics Interagency for Ministry is to build relationships, to promote dialogue, to pray and to educate the Catholic community in Australia. We work to advocate for recognition of the full equality and for justice with LGBTIQA+ Catholics, their families and friends in the Catholic Church and in our larger community. Through an interagency approach in which each Catholic organisation and group member is in an active ministry with LGBTIQA+ Catholic Christians, we celebrate the gifts, the experiences, the wholeness and the achievements and the journeys of LGBTQIA+ members of our Catholic communities, affirming their faith, sexuality, gender identity and intersex status. We work towards ending homophobia, biphobia, transphobia, intersex erasure in our church and in our communities where discrimination, exclusion and prejudice occurs.[11]

---

[11] Found at Rainbow Catholics InterAgency for Ministry - Australia, October 9, 2024.

In order to assist in its ministry to LGBTIQA+ Catholics, and its wider ministry to the Australian Catholic Church, the InterAgency has developed the Australian National Rainbow Catholic Pastoral Care Guide, available on its website. This Pastoral Care Guide provides a benchmark for use in Catholic organisations aspiring to be fully inclusive of LGBTIQA+ people and realities.[12]

Any individual, family, group, parish, diocese, seminar, agency or other organisation within the Catholic Church genuinely seeking better understanding and appropriate action in relation to LGBTIQA+ people and their realities, would find a wealth of information and resource there.

The energy and commitment of the many LGBTIQA+ people who have given so much to the work of this agency is astonishing, including their reaching out to 'straight' Catholics and to their Church leadership. Reaching out to straight Catholics and to their Church leadership is all too often ignored or met with indifference and misunderstanding, even outright bigotry.

Chair of the InterAgency, Benjamin Oh, was invited by the Catholic Diocese of Parramatta as a participant and resource person for its Diocesan Synod in 2023.[13] Naturally nervous in entering a space

---

[12] Ibid.

[13] An overview of the Parramatta Diocesan Synod (2023) is found at: Our First Synod, Diocese of Parramatta (parracatholic.org) October 21, 2024. The author was present at this Synod.

where Catholics from all corners of the Diocese were gathered, he found both welcome and openness at the round table he was invited to join during the meeting.

The Diocese has put in place an effective support group for LGBTIQA+ Catholics for several years with both lay and clergy as members.

Ally Network, Australian Catholic University (ACU)

Ally was founded at the ACU by staff member historian Noah Riseman, himself a 'gay' man. The University Framework 'Gender Equality, Diversity and Inclusion Framework 2021 – 2025', expresses the University's commitment to the full inclusion of and respect for members of the University community who identify as LGBTIQA+.

> The Ally Network at Australian Catholic University is a visible network of staff who support the university's pastoral commitment to providing a safe, inclusive and respectful environment for students and staff who identify as being lesbian, gay, bisexual, transgender, intersex or queer, or as having any other sexuality or gender diverse identity (LGBTIQ+).[14]

> The Ally Network operates within the context of the mission and identity of ACU as a Catholic university, and as an expression of the university's mission to act in truth and love, enhance human dignity, and serve the common good.

It would be fair to say that many of Australia's Catholic clergy and people 'in the pews' have no idea that LGBTIQA+ ministry is alive and passionately 'on mission' through agencies such as this. It has been and remains a work that is somewhat reminiscent of a missionary Church 'underground' in countries where the Church has been 'silenced'.

---

[14] Found at: GEDI Framework 2021-2025 (acu.edu.au).

Religious Orders

There are numerous other networks who work for LGBTIQA+ justice and inclusion in the Catholic Church and beyond. Among these are religious orders, both individually and collaborating through the umbrella organisation Catholic Religious Australia (CRA), working for justice and for full inclusion in the life of the Church for the most marginalised groups, including LGBTIQA+ Catholics.[15]

Public Juridic Persons (PJPs)

The Edmund Rice Education Australia (EREA) organisation is a governance and administrative body resourcing 55 former Christian Brothers schools across Australia. It is an example of what is called in Catholic Canon Law, a 'Public Juridic Person' (PJP). That is, an organisation founded to carry on the good works formerly governed and led by a religious order, in this case the Christian Brothers.[16] PJPs have full Canonical status within the Catholic Church.

EREA states in its 'Four Touchstones' document under 'Inclusive Community':

> Our community is accepting and welcoming, fostering right relationships and committed to the common good, and therefore an Edmund Rice school 'welcomes and values all members of the school community regardless of religion, race, disability, gender, sexual orientation or economic situation.'[17]

Other examples of PJPs include Good Samaritan Education, Kildare Ministries and Dominican Education Australia (DEA). The Child Safety Policy for Dominican Education, for example, reads:

---

[15] The website gives detail about the aims and projects of CRA. Found at: Catholic Religious Australia October 15, 2024.

[16] For information about Public Juridic Persons, the website of the Association of Ministerial PJPs is an excellent resource. Found at: About MPJPs - Association of Ministerial PJPs (ampjp.org.au), October 12, 2024.

[17] The full Charter for Edmund Rice Education Australia includes the four 'Touchstones' and is found at EREA_Booklet 2017_Print.indd, October 12, 2024.

'DEA hold that the care, safety and wellbeing of children, young people and adults at risk is founded on our Catholic belief that each person is made in the image and likeness of God and therefore is worthy of infinite love and respect, and [that] young people are respected, their voices are heard, and they are safe and feel safe. Particular attention is given to the needs of vulnerable children and young people, including those who identify as lesbian, gay, bisexual, transgender or intersex.'[18]

A stated policy position flags the clients to whom a Catholic organisation ministers, so that they are ready and committed to stand behind the full inclusion and guardianship of LGBTIQA+ children and their families. This is courageous and necessary given the Catholic Church's official teachings, and critical for a Church called to be on mission to bring the Good News of Christ to the world of the 21st century.

This plaque is a Welcome to LGBTQ visitors on the Reception counter at MacKillop Family Services, South Melbourne Victoria.
(Used with permission.)

---

[18] Found at: Safeguarding - Dominican Education Australia October 20, 2024

The original Ozanam House (1950s) for homeless men, and the new facility offering accommodation for the homeless, including LGBTIQA+ people through 'Pride in Place'.

The St Vincent de Paul Society: LGBTIQA+ new directions

In keeping with its commitment to its Vision and Mission in the spirit of patron St Vincent De Paul, and founder Frederic Ozanam, the St Vincent de Paul Society is constantly seeking opportunities to collaborate with other charities and governments in serving the needs of the poor and the most marginalised. These include LGBTIQA+ people.

VincentCare – an extension of the work of the St Vincent de Paul Society since 2003 in Victoria Australia – is a leading partner in a project 'Pride in Place', working with government, the Uniting Church, and community organisations. The project is a practical response to research that shows that 'Victorians who identify as lesbian, gay, bisexual, trans and gender diverse, intersex, queer or asexual are twice as likely to be at risk of, or experience, homelessness'.

The project is supporting LGBTIQA+ people across Victoria with housing, crisis accommodation or rental assistance. Ozanam House, a work of St Vincent de Paul in North Melbourne, has implemented an innovative Pride in Place project. Its website states: 'Pride in Place supports lesbian, gay, bisexual, transgender, gender diverse, intersex, asexual, and queer (LGBTQIA+) individuals in finding safe, secure, and affordable housing.'

CEO of St Vincent de Paul Society Victoria, Dr Jennifer Fitzgerald AM, commented:

> VincentCare believes equality, safety and respect are not negotiable and is proud to co-lead the Pride in Place consortium, which we know helps LGBTIQA+ community access housing in a safe and respectful way.[19]

Beyond Australia

The following are introductions to three Catholic organisations founded in the USA to minister with LGBTIQA+ Catholics and their allies. These organisations have been critical in paving the way forward for the whole Church, providing spirituality, theological research, recognition, support and advocacy. They model a future Catholicity inclusive of all.

New Ways Ministry

New Ways Ministry (NWM) was founded in 1977 in the USA by Fr Robert Nugent SDS and Sr Jeannine Gramick SSND, in response to their vision that 'lesbian and gay people could live in Church and society as equal members, free of discrimination and prejudice'.[20]

---

[19] From a feature article, 'Supporting LGBTIQA+ Victorians At Risk Of Homelessness', March 26, 2024. Found at: Supporting LGBTIQA+ Victorians At Risk Of Homelessness, Premier October, 2024. Further insight into LGBTIQA+ Youth Homeless can be found from the TED Talk '40% of Homeless Youth Are LGBTQ - What We Can Do' by Melissa Moore, April 2019. Found at: Melissa Moore: 40% of Homeless Youth Are LGBTQ - What We Can Do, TED Talk October 13, 2024.

[20] The historical development of New Ways Ministry between 1962 and 2002 is recorded in some detail in the Book of Memory published by NWM for its 25th Anniversary. This can be found at *Book_of_Memory* p. 65, (newwaysministry.org). The quotation cited here is from this booklet.

The Core Commitments are expressed in 2024 as:

- Promoting dialogue and reconciliation grounded in the unity and diversity of the Body of Christ (I Cor 12:12)
- Becoming anti-racist in our programming, publications, and internal operations
- Supporting research and resources that empower pastoral ministers and educators to advance an intersectional understanding of gender identity and sexuality
- Fostering holiness and wholeness within the Catholic LGBTQ+ community and allies through spiritual programs and resources[21]

NWM has arguably been among the most well-known and quoted Catholic organisations globally in support for LGBTIQA+ ministry. Over time, it has suffered attacks from Church leadership, and its founders were ordered to be silenced by the Vatican. However, the work of pastoral support, research and advocacy has flourished, its reach and influence steadily growing during its almost fifty years of existence. The Synod on Synodality stopped short of inviting the NWM to be represented at the Synod on Synodality. However, Sr Jeannine Gramick has been invited several times to Rome to dialogue with Pope Francis during the later stages of his papacy.

Outreach

Outreach Ministry is an LGBTQ – lesbian, gay, bisexual, transgender, queer (or questioning) – Catholic resource organisation founded by Fr James Martin SJ, former Editor of *America* magazine, advisor to Pope Francis, and a Synod on Synodality Member for the United States. The website explains:

> We offer news, essays, resources and community for LGBTQ Catholics and those who minister with them in the Catholic Church worldwide. Outreach also highlights welcoming

---

[21] Found at: https://www.newwaysministry.org/about/ October 10, 2024.

parishes, schools and other Catholic organizations ... Outreach operates under the auspices of America Media, a Jesuit ministry, and is rooted in the love of Jesus who reached out to all those who felt excluded.[22]

The Mass for the Outreach conference of August 2024 was celebrated by Cardinal Wilton Gregory of Washington, who said in his homily:

> The presence and the pastoral needs of our LGBTQ sisters and brothers may often be viewed as a volatile topic, but they must be faced with sincerity and genuine compassion. I pray that this conference advances that goal and makes us a stronger, holier and more welcoming church and nation.

Pope Francis sent a positive message and promise of prayers to the conference and this support and recognition may be seen as positive signs of a growing openness of Church leadership to ministry with LGBTQ Catholics.[23]

Dignity USA: Building an LGBTQIA+ Catholic Church

Founded in 1959, Dignity is the oldest Catholic organisation of its kind. Its vision for the integration of LGBTQIA+ Catholics has an emphasis as well on anti-racism:

> Dignity USA envisions and works for a time when lesbian, gay, bisexual, transgender, queer, intersex, and asexual Catholics and their allies are affirmed and experience dignity through the integration of their spirituality with their sexuality and/or

---

[22] Found at: https://outreach.faith/

[23] Found At: https://outreach.faith/2024/08/pope-francis-united-in-prayer-with-outreach-lgbtq-catholic-conference/

gender identity, and [who] can participate fully in all aspects of life within the Church and society as beloved persons of God. We uphold anti-racism as an essential part of our ethos and recognize that every individual possesses inherent dignity by virtue of being created by God, redeemed by Christ, and sanctified by the Holy Spirit through Baptism.[24]

As mentioned earlier in this chapter, Dignity sponsored the young LGBTQIA+ Catholics who attended World Youth Day 2023. Dignity has a track record of commitment to addressing both internal Church issues impacting LGBTQIA+ Catholics, and action in the public square, for example in relation to health care, asylum and migration challenges and foster care.

In 2015, Dignity assisted in the founding of the Global Network of Rainbow Catholics.

Dignity NY, November 2, 2024, used with permission.

Global Network of Rainbow Catholics

The five 'Key Goals and Objectives' of Global Network of Rainbow Catholics give an indication of the reach across the globe of this umbrella network, and the breadth of its brief, in attempting to link

---

[24] Found at: https://www.dignityusa.org/ October 10, 2024.

the many Catholic groups around the world committed to justice for all those suffering exclusion from the Church. As well as the focus on LGBTIQA+ people, the Network focus includes full inclusion of women. Their five goals are:

- **PROPHECY AND JUSTICE**
  Lifting up the voices of LGBTIQA+ people, and all who are marginalised in the Catholic Church and in society.

- **DIALOGUE**
  Connecting LGBTIQA+ Catholics with one another and with the wider church.

- **INCLUSION**
  Respect for the different cultural experiences that LGBTIQA+ people encounter across the globe, connecting and resourcing them.

- **SPIRITUALITY AND FAITH DEVELOPMENT**
  Sharing our spiritualities, sensibilities and faith with one another, with other LGBTIQA+ people and the whole church. We strive to educate Catholic leadership, institutions, and audiences about the spiritual gifts that LGBTIQA+ people bring to the Church.

The Growing importance of Catholic LGBTIQA+ groups as agents of change

Unfortunately, most Catholics are unaware of these committed organisations that identify as faithfully 'Catholic' and have been found to work for the full dignity, acceptance and inclusion of LGBTIQA+ people within their Church. It is heartening that the groundwork

for reform and renewal of the whole Church is being laid by these groups. Even more encouraging is the growing recognition by the hierarchical leadership of the Church that they are important sources for the education and mentoring of those who will need to be agents of necessary change to Canon Law and Church doctrines. Some Canons and doctrines are clearly archaic and discriminatory. Wise, well-informed leadership is needed to address this challenge. As Pope Francis has recognised, who better than the Catholic LGBTIQA+ agencies to assist and advise Church leadership and provide support in developing education and formation for both clergy and laity?

> As Pope Francis has recognised, who better than the Catholic LGBTIQA+ agencies to assist and advise Church leadership and provide support in developing education and formation for both clergy and laity?

Catholic LGBTIQA+ people engaged in action for justice in the public square

Tasmanian gay man Julian Punch – an ordained priest no longer in formal official Church ministry – is an LGBTIQA+ advocate who has worked all his adult life in ministering to those on the margins of society, particularly those who identify as LGBTIQA+. His extraordinary life of commitment makes fascinating reading.[25]

Julian is President of the organisation 'Rainbow Communities Tasmania Inc.', which aims to 'effect changes in community attitudes and policies ensuring that sexual and gender diversity is acknowledged and valued'.

---

[25] Punch J, *Gay with God: The life and times of a turbulent priest*, self-published, Australia, 2017.

Supporting LGBTIQA+ people fleeing persecution

Rainbow Communities Tasmania has an active project working in collaboration with other Human Rights advocates including Sydney law expert Chris Sidoti, a former Australian Human Rights Commissioner.

This project aims to assist LGBTIQA+ asylum seekers and refugees fleeing persecution and even potentially death, to gain safety in Australia or another country. In their countries homosexuality remains a criminal offence and they live in fear of being detected and reported. Julian told of two homosexual men who had been arrested and beheaded in Iran.

He shared the story of a young man in Bangladesh who phoned him out of the blue asking for help, having searched the internet and found Rainbow Communities Tasmania. Julian visited him in Dakka, and has since supported him in gaining higher education in the UK. Julian finds great fulfilment in his life after having come to terms with his own sexuality after years of anger and rejection. The work in collaboration with the Australian Immigration Department and international agencies to broker visas and freedom for people like that young man 'makes me happy' he said simply, and is 'a grace from God'.[26]

PRAYERFUL CONVERSATION

- From the account above, in what sense was Julian a bearer of good news to those who are discriminated against?
- What is an example of new learning for you and stays with you after reading this chapter?

---

[26] Interview with the author, October 18, 2024.

REFLECTION

Mark 16:15

He said to them,
'Go into all the world
and preach the gospel
to all creation.'

Spend some moments of quiet reflection about what 'good news' this passage might be calling us to 'preach' in our contemporary world.

SHARED PRAYER

*Lord Jesus,
we pray that we may be bearers
of your Gospel to our LGBTIQA+ siblings
through our love for their dignity,
and our respect for their need
to find a home in society and in the Church.
We ask your blessing
on all those working
to change cultural attitudes
of bigotry and exclusion
towards people who suffer rejection
because of who they are.*

Conclusion

We can see that there has been a half century of commitment, research, solidarity, recognition, and advocacy on the sidelines of the Church, preparing the way for new consciousness and positive change.

In Chapter 3, we consider the richness of the Rainbow as a key symbol for LGBTIQA+ people and movements, and for humanity in general. The rainbow is also an important symbol in the Bible, a sign of the binding Covenant of love between the Divine Creator and humankind.

Chapter 3

The Rainbow: *Symbol and Spectrum*

Why this fascinating sign in the heavens is an important biblical and universal cultural symbol and how it became a powerful sign of hope for LGBTIQA+ movements globally. Sexual diversity in Creation as an 'ecological' question.

THE RAINBOW OF GOD'S CREATION

The rainbow, one of the most beautiful and mystical phenomena in the natural world, is beloved of LGBTIQA+ organisations and causes. How many times have we stood in awe to experience the shimmering beauty of that spectrum of refracted light across the sky?

The importance of the rainbow as a symbol (sign) of something very significant is evident across cultures and times.

A Biblical symbol of relationship between God and humankind

In Chapter 9 verses 12–15 of the Book of Genesis in The Bible, after the waters of the great flood receded God renews God's Covenant (agreement) with Noah, promising:

> This is the sign of the covenant that I make between me and you and every living creature that is with you, for all future generations: I have set my bow in the clouds, and it shall be a sign of the covenant between me and the earth. When I bring clouds over the earth and the bow is seen in the clouds, I will remember my covenant that is between me and you and every living creature of all flesh, and the waters shall never again become a flood to destroy all flesh.

THE RAINBOW: SYMBOL AND SPECTRUM

This passage from Genesis is read in every Catholic Church liturgy for the First Sunday of Lent.

Is there connection between God's promises of fidelity to Creation, and the significance of the rainbow for LGBTIQA+ people?

LGBTQ lay ministry leader John Huân Vu, from the Catholic Diocese of San José in the USA, wrote a reflection, 'What Are Your Covenants (Under God's Rainbow) this Lent?' Published for New Ways Ministry, the reflection touched on the importance of this passage from Genesis for LGBTQ people. The reflection was written in the light of John's experience while travelling in Alaska, and a visit to the small Alaskan town of Skagway. He was surprised to discover rainbows on flags, pins, posters; everyone seemed to have one or want one.

The town was celebrating its 'third annual Pride' the people explained. John tells:

> I reflected on what this whole experience meant to me. Seeing those rainbow items represented a covenant, a statement, or a promise that the little town of Skagway truly welcomes all. Those rainbows reflected the intrinsic hope that God will be with us to help humankind become inclusive, welcoming, and loving.

He concluded his reflection with these words:

> In all these years that humanity existed, God has upheld God's rainbow. Do you trust that God's covenant has been made to you and all living creatures of every kind?[1]

In Ezekiel Chapter 1:25-27, the prophet describes his vision of the Divine One in the following poetic words:

> And there came a voice from above the dome over their heads; when they stopped, they let down their wings. And above the dome over their heads there was something like a throne, in appearance like sapphire, and seated above the likeness of the throne was something that seemed like a human form. Upward from what appeared like the loins I saw, something like gleaming amber, something that looked like fire enclosed all around, and downward from what looked like the loins I saw something that looked like fire, and there was a splendour all around. Like the bow in a cloud on a rainy day, such was the appearance of the splendour all around. This was the appearance of the likeness of the glory of the Lord.

The 'likeness of the Lord' shines out, 'like the bow in a cloud' with 'splendour all around' in all of Creation, including all people across the spectrum of colours and variations that make up the human family, and in all living species, the planets, the billions of galaxies and the entire Cosmos God has made in love.

---

[1] Found at: What Are Your Covenants (Under God's Rainbow) This Lent, New Ways Ministry, October 16, 2024.

Rainbow coloured banners aloft in St Joseph's Church Newtown, Sydney. The parish has been a centre of welcome for LGBTIQA+ Catholics to meet, pray and attend Mass since 2006.[2]

The Rainbow: Symbol of equality and inclusion for nation-builder Nelson Mandela

Nelson Mandela knew the importance of inclusion and the dramatic consequences of exclusion. He lived and suffered to build what he had dreamed of for a liberated South Africa: a 'Rainbow Nation' with the most multiethnic government ever formed.

Mandela acknowledged the primary importance of the various religions and their commitment to human dignity, stating he wanted to lead a country 'stamped by East and West, by European and Asian, as well as genuine African influences'. His was a vision for humanity that encompassed all peoples. Government Ministers in his government as first black President of the Republic of South Africa included blacks, whites, coloureds, Muslims, Christians, Hindus, communists, liberals, conservatives and Indians.

---

[2] Found at: In Australia - Rainbow Colours Celebrate Acceptance, Pride, and Faith, New Ways Ministry, October 15, 2024.

THE RAINBOW OF GOD'S CREATION

The South African Constitution was radical for its time, ruling out all discrimination against 'race, gender, sex, pregnancy, marital status, ethnic or social origin, colour, sexual orientation, age, disability, religion, conscience, belief, culture, language and birth'. Eleven official languages were welcomed in public life. A 'rainbow' nation – an example of radical inclusion.[3]

Nelson Mandela

The Rainbow Serpent in Aboriginal mythology

Arguably, every primary school in Australia has introduced the symbol of the Rainbow Serpent to students as a sacred part of Aboriginal and Torres Strait Islander peoples' culture. This symbol is often depicted on school buildings and community gathering places as a recognition of First Nations, and a sign of possibility for unity in this country.

The vast work by leading Australian artist Sydney Nolan, 'The Snake', found at The Museum of Old and New Art (MONA) in Hobart, is a star attraction for visitors from all around the world.

The history and cultural significance of this symbol and the way in which it has been widely appropriated – often with ignorance of its real origins and significance – calls for dialogue with First Nations People and deep learning for multi-cultural modern Australia. However, there is no doubt that the Rainbow Serpent has developed symbolic importance and connection for many Australians, as a symbol of Indigenous spirituality and belief deserving of our respect.[4]

---

[3] Hallengren, Anders, 'Nelson Mandela and the rainbow of culture', article, Sept. 11, 2001. Published on the Nobel Prize website on the occasion of Mandela's reception of the prize. Found at: Nelson Mandela and the rainbow of culture - NobelPrize.org

[4] Edited extract 'creation, destruction and appropriation - the powerful symbolism of the Rainbow Serpent', by Shino Konish, taken from Symbols of Australia: Imagining a Nation, edited by Melissa Harper and Richard White. Found on The Conversation at: Friday essay: creation, destruction and appropriation - the powerful symbolism of the Rainbow Serpent (theconversation.com) October 10, 2024.

Pied Beauty

Glory be to God for dappled things –

For skies of couple-colour as a brinded cow;

For rose-moles all in stipple upon trout
   that swim;

Fresh-firecoal chestnut-falls; finches' wings;

Landscape plotted and pieced – fold, fallow,
   and plough;

And all trades, their gear and tackle and trim.

All things counter, original, spare, strange;

Whatever is fickle, freckled (who knows
   how?)

With swift, slow; sweet, sour; adazzle, dim;

He fathers-forth whose beauty is past
   change:

Praise him.

Gerard Manley Hopkins, 1864

A popular symbol

The rainbow can symbolise peace, hope, good fortune, (and the mythical bucket of gold is said to be found at its end, guarded by Irish leprechauns!). A rainbow promises calm after the storm, connection between heaven and earth. The song 'Somewhere Over the Rainbow' from the film *The Wizard of Oz* is one of the most whimsical and popular of all time, standing for dreams for a future of one's own.

The Rainbow flag: LGBTIQA+ Universal Symbol

Around the world, the Rainbow flag has become the unifying symbol for Gay Rights. It was designed in 1978 by gay man Gilbert Baker. The flag, recognised now across the world, includes six colours: red for life, orange for healing, yellow signifying sunlight, green for nature, indigo for harmony, and finally violet for spirit.

Baker decided to make that symbol a flag because he saw flags as the most powerful symbol of pride for nations and for recognisable identity. As he later said in an interview:

THE RAINBOW: SYMBOL AND SPECTRUM

Our job as gay people was to come out, to be visible, to live in the truth, as I say, to get out of the lie. A flag really fits that mission, because that's a way of proclaiming your visibility or saying, 'This is who I am!'

Baker saw the rainbow as a natural flag from the sky.[5]

Making the connections

It would not be too great a stretch for Christians to reflect on the potential connections between the six concepts symbolised by the colours of the flag, and the teachings of Jesus.

- Red for Life: 'I am the Way, the Truth and the Life' (John 14:6)
- Orange for Healing: 'Come to me all who labour and are heavy burdened and I will give you rest' (Matthew: 11:28)
- Yellow for Sunlight: 'I am the Light of the world' (John 8:12)
- Green for Nature: 'See the lilies of the field. Not even Solomon in all his glory was arrayed like one of these' (Matthew: 6:25)
- Blue for Harmony: 'May they be one Father, as you and I are one. May they be one in us' (John: 17:21)
- Violet for Spirit: 'The Holy Spirit will teach you all things' (John: 14:25)

Believers from other faith traditions could likewise seek out connections between their own values and beliefs and the values signified by the colours of the LGBTIQA+ international flag.

In the final chapter we consider what more the Catholic Church needs to do to become a true 'home' for all the baptised, and a sign of love, recognition and embrace of LGBTIQA+ people as images of God.

---

[5] Gonzalez, Nora Gonzalez, 'How Did the Rainbow Flag Become a Symbol of LGBTQ Pride?', article, Britannic. Found at: How Did the Rainbow Flag Become a Symbol of LGBTQ Pride?, Britannica, October 11, 2024.

REFLECTION

'The various colours came to reflect both the immense diversity and the unity of the LGBTQ community.'

PRAYFUL CONVERSATION

- What can we understand by the 'immense diversity' of LGBTIQA+ people? And their 'unity'?
- What new learning is there in reading about the origins of the Rainbow Flag?

PRAYER

*May life in abundance be experienced
by all in God's human family.
May the healing hands of Jesus extend over
those who suffer misunderstanding.
May the sunshine of goodness and kindness
shine warmth on our relationships.
May the Loving Creator be praised
for the beauty and wonder of the natural
world around us.
May families and communities be blessed
with harmony and peace.
Come Holy Spirit fill the hearts of your faithful
and kindle in them the fire of your Love.*

Chapter 4

Where to from here for the Catholic Church?

We explore the processes of dialogue, deep listening and theological development. We draw on real life experience, openness to new learning and the guidance of the Holy Spirit. All are necessary in shaping the Church's relationship with LGBTIQA+ people, and at last fully recognising their innate God-given human dignity.

THE RAINBOW OF GOD'S CREATION

There were many Catholics who hoped that the Synod on Synodality would provide a breakthrough in the Church's teaching and practice regarding LGBTIQA+ people. This so-called 'hot-button issue' had been entrusted to one of the ten 'Study Groups' commissioned by Pope Francis for further study outside the Synod process, and it remained off limits from the official Synod agenda. However, the issue remained alive and urgent in the hearts and minds of many delegates and interested Catholics.

This chapter sets out some ways in which the Church is called to ramp up its dawning awareness that Catholic teaching and practice regarding LGBTIQA+ persons and issues must be seriously addressed. The time is ripe.

Open dialogue with LGBTIQA+ Catholics

During the second session of the Synod (October 2024), Fr James Martin SJ, founder of Outreach, organised a 'Dialogue' with LGBTIQA+ Catholics. That was held in the Jesuit Generalate just outside the walls of the Vatican. The event provided an opportunity for open dialogue, while denied a presence inside the Synod Hall itself where consideration of this reality had no official place on the agenda.

Synod members attended, including some Cardinals. Countries represented included Uganda, Zimbabwe, Malta, Chile, the United Kingdom and the United States. Five panellists shared their responses to these questions: 'What do you love about the Catholic Church? Who is Jesus to you? What do you want synod delegates to know about your experience as an LGBTQ Catholic?'[1]

Among the powerful responses shared, Dumisani Dube, a Zimbabwe-born gay Catholic human rights activist from South Africa, described the Catholic Church as his 'family':

> I am here to stay. I've learned that faith and identity are not mutually exclusive, and that God's love is wide enough

---

[1] O'Loughlin, Michael J, 'LGBTQ Catholics share their stories at the Synod', article. Found at: LGBTQ Catholics share their stories at the Synod, in Outreach October 15, 2024.

to encompass every part of me. For anyone facing the same struggles, know that you are not alone, and that both your faith and your identity are sacred.²

An African panellist expressed regret that countries on his continent were not heeding the call of Pope Francis to decriminalise homosexuality. A woman stated that she just wanted acceptance and the chance to 'continue to serve her Church'. Another said that the love of Jesus can show the Church that LGBTQ Catholics are 'human beings' rather than 'the summation of their sins.'³

It was an event that modelled the 'synodal' approach, commented James O'Loughlin, CEO of Outreach who reported on the event. He found the conversation 'contemplative and respectful' and 'that it happened at all showed a spirit of dialogue has taken hold in Rome.'⁴

A gathering of this kind is an example of how opportunities for dialogue enable the Church to meet face-to-face with LGBTIQA+ people and hear directly what it has been like to live their lives within or beyond the Church.

Dialogue needs to happen not only at the highest level of the Church but in parishes, dioceses and Church organisations such as hospitals, schools, charities like the St Vincent de Paul Society and religious orders.

> I am here to stay. I've learned that faith and identity are not mutually exclusive, and that God's love is wide enough to encompass every part of me. For anyone facing the same struggles, know that you are not alone, and that both your faith and your identity are sacred.
>
> Dumisani Dube

---

2   White, Christopher, 'LGBTQ issues surface inside and outside the Vatican', article, National Catholic Reporter, October 10, 2024. Found at: 'LGBTQ issues surface inside and outside the Vatican', search (bing.com)

3   Ibid.

4   Ibid.

Jesuit Generalate in Rome just outside the Vatican walls

Global online dialogue

Further examples of dialogue in action are the webinars that have become common among Catholic renewal and reform groups within Oceania and other continents since COVID.

One such opportunity was taken up by thousands of viewers in 2023 when the Australasian Catholic Coalition for Church Reform (ACCCR), Rainbow Catholics InterAgency for Ministry, Garratt Publishing, Yarra Theological Union, the University of Divinity and Catholic Religious Australia, all presented an online dialogue with gay theologian Fr James Alison, speaking on **How did we get here: LGBTIQA+ and the Church?**

The Responder from Acceptance WA, Angela Han, is a lay LGBTIQ Catholic. A gay man, Noah Riseman, an academic from the organisation Ally at the Australian Catholic University, facilitated the Question-and-Answer session.

For many among the thousands of viewers this was the first time they had heard and encountered first-hand LGBTIQA+ Catholics speaking and sharing their experience in a public forum.[5]

---

[5] Found at: JAMES ALISON - How did we get here: LGBTIQA+ and the Church? (youtube.com)

WHERE TO FROM HERE FOR THE CATHOLIC CHURCH?

Dialogue during the Synod on Synodality second session 2024

Online Synod press briefings from the Vatican Media Office provided daily opportunities for both updates and dialogue with a facilitated panel of Synod members. This was followed by questions, and streamed live to the world. For those wanting to follow and report on the Synod globally from outside the Synod Hall, these were golden opportunities, an example of how Pope Francis moved in practical ways to engage with the world.

During the press briefing on the Synod theme 'Care of Relationships'[6] Francis DeBernado, Executive Director for New Ways Ministry, seized the moment and posed a question on behalf of New Ways Ministry and LGBTIQA+ Catholics. This brought them into the ambit of the Synod through this forum. Panellists Cardinal Joseph Tobin (USA), European theologian Dr Giuseppina De Simone, and Bishop Shane McKinlay (Australia) were invited to respond.

DeBernardo first acknowledged that Cardinal Tobin was well known for his pastoral support of LGBTIQA+ Catholics. Then he asked whether any changes to LGBTQ issues, in tone or approach, had occurred during the year since the first 'very difficult' 2023 Synod. The panellists each responded, pointing out that, despite the Synod ban on formal discussion as part of the Synod agenda, discussion about LGBTIQA+ issues had happened both in and outside the Synod Hall. The Cardinal strongly advised LGBTIQA+ Catholic advocates, not once, but twice, with the words 'Don't go away!', even if they were feeling 'unsatisfied'.

The 'claims' being made by LGBTIQA+ Catholics and their supporters are gradually being better understood. Bishop McKinlay commented, and it is important to understand that LGBTIQA+ issues are seen differently in the diverse cultural contexts of a universal Church.

---

[6] Article, 'Synod Briefing Day 9', found at: Synod Briefing - Day 9: Care of relationships - Vatican News October 11, 2024. Also the article, 'At Synod, U.S. Cardinal Tells LGBTQ+ Catholics and Allies: 'Don't Go Away', Robert Shine (he/him), New Ways Ministry, October 12, 2024. Found in At Synod, U.S. Cardinal Tells LGBTQ+ Catholics and Allies: 'Don't Go Away', New Ways Ministry.

Cardinal Joseph W Tobin CSsR (USA) and Francis DeBernardo, Executive Director, New Ways Ministry, Maryland, USA.

Blessing gay unions

Cardinal Tobin reminded the panel that Pope Francis had 'gone ahead' since the 2023 Synod session by continuing to dialogue with LGBTIQA+ people and agencies. Moreover, in November 2023 he had promulgated the Vatican Declaration, '*Fiducia Supplicans*: On the Pastoral Meaning of Blessings' which included blessings for LGBTIQA+ loving unions.[7] This has proved to be a source of joy for many Catholics and a source of strong resistance to others, including some in Church leadership, especially in African countries. In summary, the message was that in the absence of an opportunity for open dialogue within the Synod about LGBTIQA+ matters, there remained much interest both inside and outside the Synod, and much work is to be done.

The consistent message from Synod participants and Synod leadership remains clear: the key to advancing this very important reality for the Church, as with all sensitive, pressing concerns and issues, lies in the Synodal way of respectful listening, prayerful conversations and the integrity of dialogue.

---

[7] Document found at: Declaration Fiducia Supplicans On the Pastoral Meaning of Blessings (18 December 2023) (vatican.va) Oct 12, 2024.

The importance of research
Finding a methodology: 'See, Judge, Act' meets the Synodal way

If change is to come, professional research in relation to this challenging reality is needed as a base of inquiry to more fully understand the need for change. Pope Francis, in his pastoral responses and his writing of the great encyclicals, has favoured the Catholic 'See, Judge, Act' methodology of Cardinal Joseph Cardijn which is still alive in the worldwide movement of the Young Catholic Workers (YCW) which Cardijn founded in 1912 in Belgium.

The first step in this method is to 'See' a situation, which involves engaging in both qualitative and quantitative methods of inquiry.

Qualitative, as the term implies, means spending quality time observing, interviewing, surveying, gathering, meeting and sharing actual human experience on the ground in the context of people's daily lives, and then engaging with them in openness and deeply respectful attention. In shorthand, qualitative data involves hearing the 'stories' that comprise human experience.

We know how often Pope Francis made a practice of meeting with people to learn about their lives and problems, and how he urged Catholics to engage face-to-face with those human beings who live 'on

Round tables at the Synod on Synodality: powerful symbols of dialogue, equality and deep listening

the peripheries' (the outer edges of the planet and of so called 'western' cultures). The Cardinals Pope Francis appointed from countries and contexts like Fiji, Mongolia, Papua New Guinea, Myanmar, Mexico and the Ukrainian Orthodox Church, reflected his commitment to bringing those on the 'outer' into the centre of the Church.

Currently the 'periphery' includes LGBTIQA+ Catholics who have been 'on the outer' in their Church.

Different to the qualitative, quantitative research collects data about people and situations that is numerical, and is reported in mathematical expressions, for example statistics, graphs, charts, tables and percentages.

The National Centre for Pastoral Research (NCPR), an agency of the Catholic Bishops of Australia,[8] engages in extensive research and reports regularly to the Bishops and the wider Church on its findings. Aspects of Church culture such as the ethnic backgrounds of Catholics, and the changing numbers of practising and non-practising Catholics, are the subject of reports, presented through both qualitative and quantitative data.

A comprehensive study into the lives and needs of LGBTIQA+ Catholics is much needed to inform the Church of their experience as minority groups both in society and Church, and how the Church needs to respond. The NCPR has demonstrated that it would be more than capable of carrying out such research in Australia to inform the Bishops and the whole Church in their discernment about this challenging area that presents such a stumbling block.

Data from the Plenary Council and the Synod on Synodality

The vast amount of consultative feedback from both the Australian Plenary Council[9] and the Synod on Synodality clearly demonstrates the deeply felt desire of the People of God to see the Church

---

[8] Found at: National Centre for Pastoral Research (NCPR) % (catholic.org.au), October 2024.

[9] 'The Document, 'Listen to what the Spirit is Saying': Final Report for the Plenary Council Phase 1: *Listening and Dialogue'*, 2019, is available at: Listen to What the Spirit is Saying , accessed on October 12, 2023.

recognise and include LGBTIQA+ people as full expressions of God's Creation, equal in dignity with all the Baptised who make up the Church membership.

The Plenary Council Report stated, 'Overall, a substantial number of submissions received were on the theme of same-sex attracted persons. Within such submissions, many participants specifically called for outreach to same sex-attracted persons.' One respondent wrote:
Following the same-sex marriage debate, how can we reach out to members of the LGBTI+ community who are practising Catholics, welcoming them back to a supportive Church
(p. 125, Chapter 10, Outreach.)

Listen to what the Spirit is Saying: Final Report for the Plenary Council, Phase 1 - Listening and Dialogue

The amount of qualitative feedback received forms a huge body of research material. The first Report, 'Listen to what the Spirit is saying' ran to 298 pages. This has been the effort of the Australian Catholic Bishops' National Centre for Pastoral Research, and represents years of work and massive expenditure of time, effort and resources.

The Synod on Synodality has been dubbed the largest consultation process undertaken in history, and extended across three levels of consultation: within dioceses, within nations and within each of the six continents.

The Catholic people who contributed in their hundreds of thousands to both the Plenary Council and the Roman Synod, deserve to have their contributions taken seriously, resulting in positive outcomes. There has indeed been much evidence available for the Church to SEE clearly.

In scriptural language the Church needs now to utilise the data to 'produce fruits that will last' (John 15:16). These 'fruits' include due attention to the dignity and inclusion of LGBTIQA+ people.

Other research

Important research projects, independent of the Vatican, have added to the data available to the Church and to society, enabling LGBTIQA+ realities to be 'seen' for what they are.

For example, in preparation for the Synod on Synodality, the Latin LGBTIQ Catholics of the Global Network of Rainbow Catholics (GNRC) developed a *Survey on Inclusive Latin LGBTIQ Catholics*. Its purpose was to investigate the experiences of LGBTIQA+ Catholics and their allies in the Catholic Church. More than 800 Latin LGBTIQ Catholics and interested people responded. The findings provide valuable insights for the first time into the experience and challenges for Latin LGBTIQ Catholics and their supporters. Among the findings were:

- 98% of those who answered the survey identified with the LGBTIQA+ community, or were allies or people who would like to see a more positive approach towards the Rainbow Catholic community in the wider Church.
- 33% of respondents shared that they only sometimes feel themselves as part of the Church. An additional 6% argued that they do not feel part of the Church.

GNRC commented that this research raises many questions for Catholics and Catholicism. These include:

– Where does the message of love and embrace get lost?

– What makes this particular community feel different from the rest?[10]

These questions can be taken on board by the wider Church as it discerns how to move forward from where we are.

---

[10] Found at: Survey on Latin LGBTIQ Catholics for the Synod, Global Network of Rainbow Catholics

> ## REFLECTION
>
> *At its Assembly in Parramatta, July 2024, The Uniting Church of Australia put forward a proposal inviting 'Affirmation for transgender, intersex and gender-diverse people'.*
>
> In the words of its proposal, the Assembly 'seeks to affirm, welcome and honour the life and faith of transgender, intersex and gender diverse people in our Church'. Assembly members agreed to recognise that transgender, gender diverse and intersex people are beloved by God and full members of the Body of Christ in baptism and resolved to 'invite congregations and councils of the Church to welcome and honour transgender, gender diverse, and intersex people, and the gifts and skills they bring to all aspects of the Church's life, including worship, leadership, and social justice advocacy.'[11]
>
> *Reflect on the above initiative from another Christian denomination, asking prayerfully, 'What can Catholics learn from this proposal?'*

---

[11] Found at: 17th Assembly – Uniting Church Australia

THE RAINBOW OF GOD'S CREATION

> ### Prayerful Conversation
>
> - How do you respond to the results of the survey conducted by the Latin Global Network of Rainbow Catholics outlined above?
> - What could be done in countries like Australia in order to have a clear picture of how LGBTIQA+ people experience membership in the Catholic Church? (Whether as practising or non-practising Catholics.)

SHARED PRAYER

*O God, Trinity of love,
from the profound communion of your divine life,
pour out upon us a torrent of fraternal love.
Grant us the love reflected in the actions of Jesus,
in his family of Nazareth,
and in the early Christian community.*

*Grant that we Christians may live the Gospel,
discovering Christ in each human being,
recognizing him crucified
in the sufferings of the abandoned
and forgotten of our world,
and risen in each brother or sister
who makes a new start.*

Come, Holy Spirit, show us your beauty,

*reflected in all the peoples of the earth,
so that we may discover anew
that all are important and all are necessary,
different faces of the one humanity
that God so loves. Amen.*

*(This ecumenical prayer for all Christians is from Pope Francis' encyclical
Fratelli Tutti, which was published on 4 October 2020.)*

Learning through ecumenism

Part of the Church's learning and research is to be in dialogue with other faith groups who have blazed the trail of inclusion and have much important pastoral experience, new knowledge, and fresh theology to share. We ask, 'Can the Catholic Church have the humility to learn from them?'

New Learning:
Good science meets good theology

The modelling of *Laudato Si*

Prior to the launch of *Laudato Si*, the major encyclical on 'Care for or Common Home' (2015), Pope Francis consulted credible scientists on the science of climate change and the environment. These economists understood the economic impact of Earth's devastation, and the social scientists understood the impact on those people and societies most affected. Secular science and Catholic theology came together to create an integrated 'Catholic' Christian approach to the global crisis of Climate Change, finding expression in the hugely influential *Laudato Si* (2015) and seven years later, *Laudate Deum* (2023).

A similar process for LGBTIQA+ realities

A similar process is needed to bring together best knowledge from the human and physical sciences in coming to a fully informed understanding of LGBTIQA+ people within the family of humanity.

Why couldn't the Vatican Academies of Science and Human Development be commissioned to facilitate such a dialogue, bringing together medical, legal and religious specialists, in conversation with the Church's most credible theologians and Scripture scholars?

The Catholic agencies founded to minister to LGBTIQA+ Catholics and others would need to be an integral part of these processes, bringing many years of first-hand pastoral experience and acquired expertise. For example, as early as 1992, Fr Robert Nugent and Sr

Jeannine Gramick, founders of New Ways Ministry, published their ground-breaking book, *Building Bridges: Gay and Lesbian Reality and the Catholic Church*. This book laid out the scientific evidence ruling out the common belief at the time that homosexuality was a 'disorder' or a 'disease'.[12]

'Judging' rooted in faith and contemplation

The second step of the See, Judge, Act Method, is judging the importance of the data available, and *reflecting on* the realities revealed in the light of Catholic theology, Catholic Social Teaching and scriptural interpretation, accompanied by prayer for the guidance of the Holy Spirit. This important process paves the way for sound decision-making and positive change, leading to *Action*.

In this way, as the Catholic Faithful and Church leadership became exposed to LGBTIQA+ reality, the Church will be better prepared to respond to the call of the Second Vatican Council to 'Read the signs of the times'. The key document, *Gaudium et Spes*, states in Paragraph 4, '... the Church has always had the duty of scrutinizing the signs of the times and of interpreting them in the light of the Gospel'.[13]

With the guidance of the Holy Spirit, the Church could then act wisely in response to this particular 'sign' of our own times, the call for recognition of the human dignity of LGBTIQA+ people, and the inclusion of Baptised LGBGTIQA+ people as full members of the Body of Christ.

Discernment as 'an affair of the heart'

The importance of contemplation in the process of discernment is critical. Pope Francis, in *Dilexi Nos* (19), is promoting discernment as an 'affair of the heart' rather than purely of the mind. He offers the model of Mary, Christ's Mother:

---

[12] Nugent R and Gramick J, *Building Bridges: Gay and Lesbian Reality and the Catholic Church*, Twenty-Third Publications, Mystic CT, 1992, chapter 2, 'Debunking the Myths'.

[13] Found at: Gaudium et spes https://www.vatican.va/archive/hist_councils/ii_vatican_council/documents/ vat-ii_const_19651207_gaudium-et-spes_en.html

Mary saw things with the heart. She was able to dialogue with the things she experienced by pondering them in her heart, treasuring their memory and viewing them in a greater perspective. The best expression of how the heart thinks is found in the two passages in Saint Luke's Gospel that speak to us of how Mary 'treasured all these things and pondered them in her heart' (cf. Luke 2:19, 51).

Just as Mary 'treasured' and 'pondered all these things in her heart' (Luke 2:19), an expectant mother treasures and ponders the child growing within her, as is depicted in this now world-renowned carving of Mary, Mother of Jesus.[14]

'Mary of Warmun' or 'The Pregnant Mary', (circa 1983), carved by community spiritual leader, George Mung Mung, Warmun Catholic Community, Kimberley, WA. (Private photo by one who lived in Warmun and saw the statue in 1985. Permission granted.)

---

[14] This carving is featured as a colour plate in the Australian edition of the *Catechism of the Catholic Church*, St Pauls Publications, Sydney, 1994. Reproduced with the permission of the artist's family and the Warmum Community Corporation.

Theology as a sacred and evolving science

If progress is to be made in bringing the mission of Christ alive in the world, the work of competent theologians is important to inform the Church's decision-making. Mission Theology is needed in each era and context to open up the Gospel with new expressions, and to discover new manifestations of the Spirit of God alive and active in the world and the Church.

In November 2023, Pope Francis issued the *motu proprio*, *'Ad theologiam promovendam'*, reviewing the statutes of the Pontifical Academy of Theology. The document insists that certain elements suited to the mission of today are essential for sound theological study. These elements include: a culture of *dialogue and encounter* between different traditions, faiths and disciplines; *open engagement* with all within and beyond the Church; an *inductive method* that starts with the concrete situations in which people live, their *human experience* and the realities they face; and attention to *'common sense'*. Typically, the Pope insisted that theological work must have a 'Pastoral Stamp'.

Theological reflection leading to action: Women Preach

The podcast series, 'Australian Women Preach' is the initiative of Women and the Australian Church (WATAC) and The Grail. Over three years it has offered an imaginative, innovative way to live the change we need to see in the Catholic Church for the full inclusion of women in the ministry of preaching the Gospel. The women featured are theologically and scripturally literate and have deep, living commitment to their faith, including some who identify as LGBTIQA+. Women Preach ticks all the boxes for sound theologising that is inclusive and has resulted in effective action to model an aspect of the religious change needed in our time.[15]

---

[15] Found at: Australian Women Preach - Hear their voices.

> Even as a teacher in a Catholic school, for years she lived in a 'shadow world' where colleagues knew she was gay but where she had to watch her every move.

A spirituality: 'Becoming who we truly are' – temples of God, disciples of Christ

Without a spiritual, interior pathway and connection that puts us in touch with the Divine, we humans can feel ourselves alone in the universe. How much more so for LGBTIQA+ people who have often suffered shame, self-doubt, and negativity from others towards the person they are from the time they were children and into adult life. The following is a telling example from the Australian context.

> *A lesbian teacher experienced in Catholic schools related that while growing up she had gay friends who 'were assaulted' and has experienced 'people spitting in her face'. Even as a teacher in a Catholic school, for years she lived in a 'shadow world' where colleagues knew she was gay but where she had to watch her every move, like 'playing pieces on a chess board', listening to their 'conversations about their partners', and unable to 'share openly about her own life outside work'. In 2017, she changed to a school where the staff are 'amazing', and gay students are 'drawn' to confide in and be supported by her. The principal is appreciative of her outreach to these young people.*

> *She spoke of an experience she had during Mass. The Parish Priest publicly commented on the outcome of the Gay Marriage plebiscite and when she heard him begin his remarks from the pulpit, she had assumed he would speak against the 'Yes' majority vote. She got up to leave the Church not feeling she could bear to hear what he had to say. To her utter surprise she heard his words to the assembly, 'How did the vote go? Well, if we didn't vote 'Yes', what kind of Christians are we?' She was moved to tears. When she subsequently married her partner, the priest attended their wedding and has remained a friend and an expression of Christ's love for herself and her wife ever since.*[16]

---

[16] Interview with the author, 12 October 2024.

This incident shows how fragile and risky life can be for people who are constantly receiving a message that they are inadequate, too 'different', not fully acceptable. Once they are accepted and loved for who they are, treated with respect, supported and befriended, they have the chance to flourish and develop confidence and joy, and the ability to live life fully.

Imago Dei

Underlying this joy and new found strength, for people of Christian faith there is in fact a dawning realisation that they are an *'imago dei'*, an 'image' of God, a precious expression of God's Creation, mirroring the Love of God – God's 'work of art' – as St Paul expresses it in Ephesians 2:10.

Pastoral theologian and writer Larry Kent Graham sets out to explore in his study of gay and lesbian Christians[17] the extreme importance and empowerment for them of discovering the *'imago dei'* of their own unique nature. They are not 'damaged goods' as had so often been signalled to them. Or, as a popular poster in the years after Vatican II proclaimed, 'God does not make junk.'

And how did these gay and lesbian people discover their status as 'mirrors' of God's own love? In every case, Graham found it was through the discovery of a deep expression of reciprocal love coming into their lives through receiving positive regard or falling in love with another human being. The positive regard led to the expression of all their potential for love, including for many, erotic love through joyous sexual union, or the deep love of friendship within a life partnership, or sharing with a soul mate or living within a loving community. All are signs of Love itself ('God *is* Love', John 4:16), healing and enlivening. Ultimately the love of 'agape', the highest form of love, the love of Christ himself, may be expressed in the 'new' person they have become. This is love that is free to be given away through practical responses to

---

[17] Graham, L, *Discovering Images of God: Narratives of care among lesbians and gays, Westminister,* John Knox Press, Kentucky, 1997.

those in most need, often without thought of reward and at great personal cost.

The Spiritual Way of inclusion not rejection

The spiritual pathway for all Christians involves both the Way of the Cross, as well as the joy of knowing that God has loved us into life and has the very 'hairs of our head counted'. It is so also for LGBTIQA+ disciples of Christ. As they strive to live according to God's will for them in their daily lives, they will encounter both joy and suffering, challenges and achievements. As baptised members, the Church needs to offer them full sacramental and pastoral support for their spiritual journey. They need to be embraced by a Christian community that recognises their human dignity and giftedness. This will often require spiritual conversion for the Church, so that it no longer adds avoidable pain to their lives by continuing to offer the bitter cup they have often had to drink, through rejection and alienation, as 'disordered' members of God's Creation.

It is almost as though these people were given a superpower, a well-founded self-belief, strong enough to build new freedom and meaning through the affirmation of true love from another, loved as themselves, as the person they 'just are'. And all 'by the grace of God', as one gay person who had experienced it for himself explained to me.

This is a spirituality that believes in the revelation of God's Love, experienced through the love of another human person or persons. It is a spirituality that acknowledges that all God has made has been seen and blessed by the Creator God as 'good', including human attraction to another human being, and its expression in the gift of erotic love, in friendship, and in altruism that is poured out in loving service. Hence genuine love can become the driving force for self-fulfilment that fills one's cup, until it 'runneth over' with more than enough to share beyond one's own needs.

Why should we be surprised at these findings, when Jesus told us that the only law that matters is two-fold: to love God with all our heart and soul and love our neighbour (i.e. anyone we encounter 'on the road' of life) as we have come to respect, accept and love our own self. No wonder it's called The Golden Rule, and finds a similar expression in all the 'great religions' of the world.

An ecological question?

A response to God's great mission of Love includes a call to 'ecological conversion', a phrase first invoked by Pope John Paul II[18] and re-invoked by Pope Francis. This 'conversion' is threefold as John Paul II explained and Pope Francis reiterates.

It is a call to respond to the Love of God (the subject of *Dilexit Nos*), a call to Love one another (the subject of *Fratelli Tutti*), and a call to love the *whole* of Creation, (the subject of *Laudato Si*). Herein lies a key to understanding a reality that has been so problematic in the Catholic Church, namely, the presence in all times and cultures of those human beings who have not fitted the majority way of being human – heterosexuality – but are no less Baptised members of the Church, and children of God.

The Catholic Church needs now to come to terms with the presence in its Baptised membership of those who are among the 'non-pathological, minority variants' within God's human family, the phrase James Alison has coined to take account of both the science and the theology that underpin the *'imago dei'* status of our LGBTIQA+ siblings.

---

[18] JOHN PAUL II , GENERAL AUDIENCE Wednesday 17 January 2001, (para. 4). Found at: 17 January 2001, John Paul II (vatican.va) Nov. 6, 2024.

Some practical actions the Catholic Church could take

The following are some actions that could help to pave the way to a better future:

1. Dialogue at local level
   Parishes and Catholic organisations could be encouraged to creatively seek ways to invite LGBTIQA+ parishioners, staff, clients, and former Catholics to a 'dialogue', at a safe respectful space where experience, hopes and needs can be expressed with a view to growing understanding and empathy, and providing the Church with advice and direction about appropriate pastoral responses.

2. Welcome at Mass
   Consider including in the welcome at parish Masses an explicit welcome for people from LGBTIQA+ and minority communities.

3. Consultation with LGBTIQA+ Catholic Organisations
   Church leaders could engage in dialogue with the 'Popular Movements' in the Church that are advocating for LGBTIQA+ realities, including Catholic agencies that are already well established. (See Chapter 2.)

4. Research
   Conduct a Catholic Church research project that could explore scientific, scriptural and doctrinal aspects of LGBTIQA+ reality, with a view to building a credible base for informed decision making towards reform and renewal of relevant Church Canons, doctrine and pastoral practice.

5. Policy Development
   Ensure that Church organisations and communities (dioceses, parishes, seminaries, schools, hospitals, charities), have clear policies that recognise LGBTQA+ rights and human dignity, taking account of civil law, and Catholic Social Teaching principles.

6. **Resources**
   Include in Church newsletters or Facebook pages positive articles to help educate Catholics about LGBTIQA+ realities and share good practice of inclusion wherever that is happening around the world in dioceses or parishes.[19]

7. **Review of Courage International**
   Review Courage International (https://couragerc.org/) in the light of both scientific/medical research and best practice and the testimony of experienced Catholics.

These are but a few practical suggestions. What is really needed now is openness, dialogue and genuine 'synodality' to continue to be exercised in the Church, empowering it to the humility and the openness needed to look squarely at the challenges we must face. As Church, we need to find what we in Australia might colloquially term 'Fair Dinkum' ways to become no longer a Church that excludes LGBTIQA+ people, in either word or action.

Let the discernment continue to gain momentum, to bring forth 'fruits' of inclusion 'that will last' in union with Christ the Master of the 'Vineyard'. May we be energised by the Spirit of God, who 'blows where it wills', beyond all the limitations of human small-mindedness and bigotry. And know that The Kingdom of God is continuing to be made visible among us as we, the Church, commit to engage in this work.

---

19   The Global Catholic Resource Centre, an independent Catholic source of resources linked to Catholic Faith, offers a wealth of information and research material, including a dedicated category 'Catholic LGBTIAQ+ Resources'. Found at: about us (globalcatholicresourcecenter.com)

REFLECTION

A reading from Pope Francis' encyclical,
Dilexi Nos (8)

Instead of running after superficial satisfactions and playing a role for the benefit of others, we would do better to think about the really important questions in life. Who am I, really? What am I looking for? What direction do I want to give to my life, my decisions and my actions? Why and for what purpose am I in this world? How do I want to look back on my life once it ends? What meaning do I want to give to all my experiences? Who do I want to be for others? Who am I for God? All these questions lead us back to the heart.

THE RAINBOW OF GOD'S CREATION

PRAYERFUL CONVERSATION

- What relevance do these words from Pope Francis have for us in wanting to understand, fully recognise and support our LGBTIQA+ siblings?

- What can we learn from the narrative above shared by the lesbian woman? Have you been invited to a same-sex marriage? How would you feel about attending such a celebration?

- Consider actions that you would like to take, or see enacted by the Church, to be in greater solidarity with our LGBTIQA+ siblings.

Pope Francis' encyclical Dilexi Nos (2004) brings to new life the traditional devotion of the 'Sacred Heart' – celebrating the unfailing, all-embracing Love of Christ for us, even to death.

WHERE TO FROM HERE FOR THE CATHOLIC CHURCH?

SHARED PRAYER

*We ask our Lord Jesus Christ
to grant that his Sacred Heart may continue
to pour forth the streams of living water
that can heal the hurt we have caused,
strengthen our ability to love and serve others,
enable us to be in solidarity with them,
and inspire us to journey together towards
a just and fraternal world.
We await that day
when we will rejoice in celebrating together
the banquet of the heavenly kingdom
in the presence of the risen Lord,
who harmonizes all our differences in the light
that radiates perpetually from his open heart.
May He be blessed forever.*

(Adapted from the final paragraph of Dilexi Nos, [220], Pope Francis, October 2024)

> I was asked by a parishioner, 'Would I give scandal by going to my nephew's same sex marriage?' I asked, 'What do you think?' After some discussion I said, 'I think you would give scandal by not going.'
>
> *(Testimony from a Catholic Priest ministering in a large Australian Parish)*

Acknowledgements

My husband Vin has been a mainstay and touchstone during the process of researching and writing this Guide. He has an intuitive appreciation of human goodness and connection. He is love unfailing and patience personified, plying me throughout with cups of tea and invaluable resources, feedback and suggestions.

Peter Confeggi, retired priest from the Parramatta Diocese, has been a source of wisdom, understanding and knowledge in guiding and assisting in bringing this work to completion. Peter's lifetime of pastoral care, deep learning and spiritual leadership, together with his joyous hope in God as the source of Life and Love, have given this work an authenticity that would not otherwise have been possible.

Many people have generously and courageously shared their knowledge and human experience with me, and I am grateful. They remain for the most part unidentified, as is necessary. However, if it were not for them, I could never have dared to venture forth. Some are exhausted from the long, incessant struggle for themselves and their LGBTIQA+ siblings to be recognised as precious creations of God. Each is a unique expression of divine artistry within the wide colourful spectrum of the vast human family. This Guide is dedicated to them and to the thousands of young people whose lives I have been privileged to experience in Catholic schools over more than fifty years. In particular, this work is dedicated to trans family member Mars in Aoteroa/New Zealand.

Bibliography

DeBernardo, F and Shine, R, *A Home for All: A Catholic Call for LGBTQ Non-Discrimination*, New Ways Ministry, Maryland, 2022.

Confeggi, P, *Memoir of a Reluctant Cleric: Weaving his world with the Word*, Huon Design and Print, Hobart, 2022.

Francis, Pope. Encyclicals, *Fratelli Tutti*, 2022, *Dilexi Nos*, Vatican City, 2024.

Gramick, J and Nugent, R, *Building Bridges: Gay and Lesbian Reality and the Catholic Church*, Twenty-Third Publications, Connecticut, 1992.

Punch, J, *Gay with God: the life and times of a turbulent priest*, self-published, Hobart, 2017.

Ruis, I and Guevarra, M, *Cornerstones: Sacred Stories of LGBTQ+ Employees in Catholic Institutions*, New Ways Ministry, Maryland, 2024.

Trujillo, Y, *LGBTQ Catholics: A Guide to Inclusive Ministry*, Paulist Press, New Jersey, 2022.

Wolf, J, ed., *Gay Priests*, Harper and Row, New York, 1989.

Synod on Synodality, Vatican City, Final Report, 2024.

Pope Francis, encyclical *Fratelli Tutti*, Vatican, 2020.

Pope Francis, encyclical *Dilexit Nos*, Vatican 2024.

Pope Francis, *The Name of God is Mercy*, Penguin Random House, 2016.

www.ingramcontent.com/pod-product-compliance
Lightning Source LLC
Chambersburg PA
CBHW070359240426
43671CB00013BA/2573